THE POCKET IDIOT'S GUIDE™ TO

Garage and Yard Sales

by Cathy Pedigo and Sonia Weiss

ALPHA

A member of Penguir

SO-BEZ-334

THE POCKET IDIOT'S GUIDE TO and Design are registered trademarks of Penguin Group (USA) Inc.

International Standard Book Number: 1-59257-082-8
Library of Congress Catalog Card Number: 2003100698

05   04   8   7   6   5   4   3   2

Interpretation of the printing code: The rightmost number of the first series of numbers is the year of the book's printing; the rightmost number of the second series of numbers is the number of the book's printing. For example, a printing code of 03-1 shows that the first printing occurred in 2003.

Printed in the United States of America

Note: This publication contains the opinions and ideas of its authors. It is intended to provide helpful and informative material on the subject matter covered. It is sold with the understanding that the authors and publisher are not engaged in rendering professional services in the book. If the reader requires personal assistance or advice, a competent professional should be consulted.

The authors and publisher specifically disclaim any responsibility for any liability, loss, or risk, personal or otherwise, which is incurred as a consequence, directly or indirectly, of the use and application of any of the contents of this book.

Most Alpha books are available at special quantity discounts for bulk purchases for sales promotions, premiums, fund-raising, or educational use. Special books, or book excerpts, can also be created to fit specific needs.

For details, write: Special Markets; Alpha Books, 375 Hudson Street, New York, NY 10014.

Contents

Appendixes

Introduction

If you had to guess, what would you name as one of the top leisure activities in the United States? Believe it or not, garage and yard sales—holding them and shopping at them—rank pretty close to the top of the list.

Not only are we a nation of pack rats, it seems we're also a nation of scavengers. We delight in selling our used stuff. We thrill to the chase and the challenge of uncovering and discovering the great bargain, the once-in-a-lifetime find, the thing we can't do without. And we love to satisfy our passions at garage sales.

Even in the era of the online auction, earth-based garage sales, rummage sales, yard sales, tag sales, and the like are still going strong. And for good reason. Not only do you not need a computer (and know how to run one) to put them on or to shop them, you get almost instant gratification when you have one. Instead of waiting until the end of an auction for your profits, you can pocket them immediately. Buyers get their goods right away, too. And there are no selling or shipping fees to incur or feedback ratings to worry about. When people shop at garage sales, they know they're buying items in "as is" condition. If they're not happy with what they bought for some reason, it will probably end up in their own garage sales at some point in time.

How to Use This Book

If you've never had a garage sale (hard to believe, but some people are rookies), this book will tell you everything you need to know to plan and operate a successful sale. If you're a seasoned hand at them, you'll learn how to make them more profitable.

There are no secrets here, just time-proven, successful steps that result in money in your pocket. A successful garage sale takes substantial time and effort, but there are practical principles here that make the effort worth it all.

For garage sale shoppers, we've included advice from master garage sale mavens for maximizing both the time and money you'll spend at garage sales. Although these sales can offer great buys for bargain hounds and treasure seekers alike, there are definitely tricks to shopping them, and you'll get the inside track on them here.

Extras

You'll also find little information boxes, or "bonus boxes," sprinkled throughout this book. These present key information and facts that you won't want to miss.

Ka-Ching!

Look to these boxes for insider tips on maximizing garage sale profits.

Trash or Treasure _____

This is where you'll find tips on buying at garage sales and some selling tips, too.

 Garage Sale Don'ts _____

Words of advice on what not to do at garage sales for both buyers and sellers.

 Insider Information _____

Real-life stories of garage sale successes and disasters.

Acknowledgments

The authors wish to thank Mary Newland, who provided some great garage sale tips from her treasure trove of knowledge, and Chris Heiska, a.k.a. The Yard Sale Queen, for graciously allowing us to use real-life stories of garage sale triumphs and tragedies from her website, www.yardsalequeen.com.

Trademarks

All terms mentioned in this book that are known to be or are suspected of being trademarks or service marks have been appropriately capitalized. Alpha Books and Penguin Group (USA) Inc. cannot attest to the accuracy of this information. Use of a term in this book should not be regarded as affecting the validity of any trademark or service mark.

A Final Word

It is possible to generate income up to $1,000 and more by the end of garage sale. Is $1,000 worth it? It sure is to most people. To do it, your sale has to be different than the typical garage sale. This book will show you how. No matter what type of sale you might be planning—a yard sale, rummage sale, estate sale, tag sale, garage sale, moving sale—you'll find plenty of practical tips and advice on these pages to help you bring in lots of extra money.

It's also possible to slash your household expenses by making garage sales a regular part of your weekend routine. Are the savings worth the time and effort? Use the strategies for successful shopping in the pages ahead and your answer will be a resounding "Yes!"

We wish you good garage sale-ing!

Getting Started: Garage Sales 101

In This Chapter

- A sale by any other name
- Exploring the garage sale culture
- Reasons for having a garage sale
- Reasons to shop at them

On any given weekend, thousands of people participate in what has become one of America's most popular pastimes—holding and shopping at garage sales. Regardless of what they're actually called— yard sales, tag sales, rummage sales, porch sales, even attic sales—these weekend events (they're almost always held on weekends, although you'll find weekday sales in certain parts of the country as well) have come to rival most other leisure pursuits for popularity. Encounter a traffic tie-up on a sunny Saturday morning, and it's a sure bet that the folks beating a path to someone's yard or garage sale are causing it.

The Lure of Garage Sales

What's behind this fascination with buying and selling used stuff? The simple answer from the seller's point of view is the chance to part with items that are no longer wanted or needed and make some quick cash while doing so. For buyers, it's the thrill of the chase, the challenge of discovering a special find or a hidden treasure. Ask any dedicated garage sale shopper why she (or he, for that matter, although women definitely outnumber men in this particular pursuit) pursues garage sales with such passion, and you'll most likely be told that it's awfully hard to stop once you've found some great bargains. Talk about your win-win situation! Garage sales epitomize the tired but true saying: One person's trash is indeed another person's treasure.

Trash or Treasure _____

Knowing what to look for at a garage sale can result in finding more than a bargain. Claire Beckman, a schoolteacher from Secaucus, New Jersey, paid $25 for a rickety old table at a tag sale. It turned out to be a rare antique worth between $250,000 and $300,000.

But ... there's a little more to garage sales than meets the eye. Frankly, there would have to be to make them so popular. It's not easy to plan and hold a successful garage sale. In fact, doing it right requires a lot of planning and preparation before the event, and an equal amount of hard work during it and even after it.

Nor is shopping at garage sales always all that pleasurable. Much like flea markets and swap meets, you have to battle the elements at lots of them. There are gusts of wind that blow dust in your face, sweltering days with 90-degree heat and 95 percent humidity that burn your skin and sap your strength, sudden rain showers that spring up out of nowhere that soak you and everything else at the sale. Getting your sneakers wet in the early morning dew at a yard sale isn't everyone's idea of fun. But garage sale aficionados take it all in stride.

The Culture of Garage Sales

Spend enough time at garage sales, or hold a few yourself, and you'll begin to get a glimpse of their deeper meaning, the "Zen" of them, if you will. Sure, there's their basic commercial aspect—people with items to sell and people with money eager to buy them. But garage sales are also a proven antidote to our throwaway society for those who care about such things. Instead of tossing undesirable items into a Dumpster, the people who hold garage sales are making a commitment—whether consciously or not—to finding new homes and users for their unwanted items. By purchasing them, buyers are completing the cycle by demonstrating their willingness to rescue these items from being dumped into landfills while they still have some life left in them.

Without getting too deep here, the people on both sides of the garage sale equation comprise a microcosm of our society that, quite simply, embraces the garage sale model, perpetuates all that it embodies, and derive a great deal of satisfaction out of keeping it going, whether they realize it or not. Everyone wins—sellers and buyers as well as the environment and our planet.

Garage Sale Socials

Our society may not be much on communal activities anymore, but you wouldn't know it by watching what goes on at garage sales. Some people do nothing else on their weekends besides scope them out. Hold one and you'll see them—they're the folks with the mini-vans bearing bumper stickers that read "I brake for garage sales." They're also the ones who wave at and chat with all of their friends who, of course, are also dedicated garage sale fanatics.

For better or worse, garage sales are social occasions, and they're events that many people not only enjoy but also look forward to. They're great ways for newcomers to get to know their neighbors, and for neighbors who aren't that close to maintain some contact with each other. Some communities support and encourage the social aspect of garage sales by organizing communitywide sales and encouraging people to participate in them.

But don't think for a minute that it's just lonely hearts, retirees, or folks on a fixed income who patronize garage sales. In reality, the people who hold and shop at garage sales will defy any type of sweeping generalities you might try to make about them. For every retiree who haggles over a 50-cent item, there's a marketing mogul or high-powered exec who can well afford to buy that item new but who likes a bargain and doesn't mind spending the time seeking it out. They might leave their SUVs, Beemers, and Benz's at home, but believe it when we say that people in all social classes and income levels both hold and shop at garage sales.

Ka-Ching!

Don't have a garage or a yard? You can sell used goods just about anywhere—on your porch, in a breezeway, basement, or attic—wherever there's enough space to display your items and have people come look at them. Only hold an indoor sale if you feel comfortable about having strangers come into your home.

Garage Sales All Around

Whether you're the one holding the garage sale or you're shopping at them, you're definitely in good company. On any given weekend during garage sale season (the warm months in colder climates, year-round in warmer climes), there are bound to be many others engaging in the same activity in your community and others like yours. While garage sales tend to be more popular in smaller communities and suburbs where there's more room to hold them comfortably, they're by no means limited to these areas.

No one knows exactly where garage sales started, or when they started, but they're clearly a variation of the sales that are traditionally held to liquidate family holdings and homesteads. Unlike these sales, however, the goal behind garage sales is to sell unwanted or unneeded items, not dispose of an entire estate. For this reason, garage sales are rarely once in a lifetime affairs. Most people who hold them do so fairly regularly, ranging from semi-annually to yearly to every couple years or so, or whenever the household clutter gets to the point that no one can stand it anymore.

The Economic Factor

Garage sales have clearly been around for some time, but they made their presence known in a big way during the inflationary years of the late 1960s. As the power of the dollar dwindled, buying and selling used goods became an accepted way to make ends meet. It also appealed to the growing number of individuals who were questioning every facet of traditional society and creating alternatives to it. To the hippies and the flower children of the 1960s, there was no shame in trading in used goods. In fact, many people during this period took great pride in finding used items that they could put to good use, just like earlier generations had done during the tough years of the depression.

By the time the economy leveled out in the late 1980s, garage sales had become so popular that few questioned the reasons for having them or shopping at them. By this point, the other reasons for the popularity of garage sales—the social factor among them—had made these sales an indelible part of America's landscape.

The Collectibles Factor

Another significant driver behind the growth and popularity of garage sales was the burgeoning interest in collectibles that began in the 1980s. As antiques became rarer, their prices put them beyond the reach of many established and would-be collectors. For people who liked to collect and couldn't afford the high-ticket items, newer objects such as lunchboxes, advertising memorabilia, depression glass, Pez dispensers, and so on were widely available and cheap.

Collecting such items also provided a nostalgic connection to the past for many collectors, especially baby boomers who have disposable income and time to invest in leisure activities. At the beginning of the collectibles craze, garage sales were one of the leading sources for these items, and collectors often were able to uncover some incredible finds put out by sellers who had no idea that their old junk was worth something more beyond its intrinsic value.

Today, sellers are generally savvier about collectibles and bargains are harder to come by. But they're still out there, and new collectibles categories crop up all the time. Collectors continue to prowl garage sales in search of undiscovered treasures that they can add to their own collections or resell to others.

Why Have a Garage Sale?

The basic reason for having a garage sale or yard sale is pretty obvious: It's a great way to get rid of things you don't want or that your family no longer needs. So what if something you own has exceeded its usefulness in your household. That doesn't mean it can't be useful in someone else's home. More often than not, there's someone out there—and often more than one someone—who would be thrilled to take that old griddle or power drill off your hands—and pay you for the privilege!

But getting rid of items that have reached their obsolescence in your home is just one of many reasons for organizing a garage sale to sell them. Here are a few more:

- **Getting ready to move.** Why spend time packing and unpacking items you'd rather leave behind? Having a garage sale might be the last thing you'll want to do when planning a move, but it's a good way to bring down relocation costs.

- **Remodeling and renovation.** You've finally turned that unused space in your basement into a bedroom, or that unused bedroom into a hobby area. Why not get rid of the old decorations and furnishings to help pay for new ones?

- **Making some quick cash.** There are few better ways to come up with some money when you're in a pinch.

- **Teaching your kids the value of a buck.** There's no reason why your kids can't help out at your garage sale, and perhaps even earn some pocket money of their own. Why not have a rule that for every new toy, doll, or stuffed animal that they get, they put an old item, maybe something they've outgrown, into the garage sale box for the next time you have a sale.

- **Paying for a family vacation.** Many families use the proceeds from their garage sales to pay for something special, such as a family trip or a high-ticket item that their regular income might not stretch far enough to cover.

- **Raising funds for a community or church group.** Rummage sales, tag sales, and the like are classic fundraisers for nonprofit groups.

- **Decluttering clutter.** Growing families generate a lot of clutter as old items lose interest or are outgrown and new items are acquired. Having regularly scheduled garage sales is a great way to keep household clutter to a manageable level, and perhaps even eliminate it!

A well-planned sale can net you $1,000 or more for a weekend's worth of work depending on the items you have to sell and such factors as the weather and your competition—other sales that are going on at the same time as yours. Even a more limited sale can easily bring in $500 or so if you plan it well and price your items right.

The Downside to Garage Sales

Although there aren't many reasons not to have a garage sale, this doesn't mean there aren't some negatives associated with them. Some people literally don't want to get rid of their stuff. For them, just the thought of parting with their treasures will put them into a traumatic tailspin. If your life is already crammed to the gills and planned to the second, the time and effort it takes to plan and hold a garage sale might seem like burdens you'd rather not shoulder.

Ka-Ching!

If you're the shy type and uncomfortable around people you don't know, consider taking a backseat role when having your garage sale. Do the planning and the organizing, and manage the money box during the sale. Let a more gregarious member of your family chat up and encourage potential buyers to dig into their pockets and open their purses.

Other less-than-savory elements of garage sales include the following:

- **Bad weather.** Cold or rainy weather can shut down even the best-planned garage sale or vastly affect turnout.

- **Seller's remorse.** Items that for one reason or another shouldn't be sold sometimes are, much to the regret of the owner. Sometimes it happens by mistake, sometimes it seems like a good idea at the time.

- **Dealing with difficult buyers.** There are a fair number of garage sale aficionados who greatly enjoy the art of the deal and who take haggling to its highest level. These people can nickel and dime you over nickel and dime items, and wear you down to the point of disgust. Shoplifting is another problem that you may have to deal with. Sad to say, it happens more frequently than it should.

- **Problems with the law.** First-time sellers sometimes assume that garage sales are unregulated activities. They are in some areas, but most communities do have regulations regarding them. Some municipalities require sellers to apply for a permit before holding garage sales. Your local government may also limit how many sales you can have during the course of a year (and how many you can have before your activities constitute a business), what you can sell, how long you can hold your sale, where you can put your signs, how many signs you can have, and when you have to take them down. Violations can be enforced with a fine, although violators usually receive nothing more than a slap on the wrist and a warning not to do it next time.

- **Problems with your neighbors.** Hard to believe, perhaps, but not everyone likes garage sales. The volume of traffic generated by a successful sale, buyers trampling over adjoining lawns, even ill-placed sale signs can cause strife even among the friendliest neighbors.

The good news is that the many garage sale downsides can easily be mitigated or eliminated. If you're having a sale during a dicey time of year when it comes to the weather, you can plan an alternative date if conditions on your sale date are inclement. Planning your sale well in advance—and asking your family to pitch in—can spread out the workload and make it easier for you to do all the things you should do to maximize your profits. Checking and rechecking with an item's owner—your kids, your husband, your sister, whomever—can lessen the chances of your getting blamed for selling cherished possessions that maybe shouldn't have been put up for sale in the first place.

Having family, friends, or neighbors help you during the sale can make it far easier to handle difficult buyers and shoplifters. Checking with local authorities and advising neighbors of your plans to have a sale can eliminate problems in both arenas before they happen.

Don't let the downsides of garage sales discourage you from having one. Be aware of the problems, plan for them, and then focus on the plus side. All the good reasons for having a garage sale just about always cancel out the bad ones.

Why Shop at Garage Sales?

Another obvious answer here: to find great bargains! If you believe in living frugally, garage sales are some of the best places to find the things to help you do it. If you have a young family, great savings can be had in buying used clothing and athletic equipment instead of new items that are rapidly outgrown. If you just got married and need to furnish your new home, take a tip from thousands of newlyweds and pick up essential and maybe not-so-essential items at a song at your local garage sales.

Bargain shopping is probably the leading reason why people make garage sales a part of their lives, but it's by no means the only one. Avid garage sale shoppers cite the following reasons as motivation behind their searches as well:

- **Finding pieces and parts for old appliances.** Such things as crock pot lids and Cuisinart bowls are easily lost or broken. If you've had the appliances they go with for a while, replacement pieces may not be available. But you might find them lurking in a box of old housewares at a garage sale.

- **Breathing new life into old goods.** The rusty old wagon you picked up for a buck at your neighbor's garage sale might see new use as a planter in your backyard garden. That incredibly ugly coffee table they literally pleaded with you to take off their hands? With a fresh coat of paint and new pulls on the drawers, it can turn into a snazzy addition to your downstairs den.

Ka-Ching! _____

As more and more people turn to gardening as a leisure time activity, old tools and other items that can be used to accessorize garden areas have increased in value. Check the prices in a collectibles guide or online before putting them in your sale. Don't worry about cleaning these pieces—the rust and patina they've developed over time add to their charm.

- **Discovering hidden treasures.** Although it's become more difficult to find valuable collectibles at garage sales, it can still happen. It's also possible to find highly valuable pieces at garage sales that have clearly escaped the seller's eye. Stories about buyers finding jewelry worth thousands of dollars (and paying next to nothing for it) are very numerous.

- **Finding unusual or hard-to-come-by arts and crafts materials.** Old buttons, yarn, beads, antique fabric, thread, paint—you name it and you'll probably find it at a garage sale—and for far less than what you'd pay at your local hobby shop.

Always remember that it's possible to find just about anything at a garage sale. You may come away from some searches empty-handed, but keep at it and you'll greatly improve the chances of your locating exactly what you're after.

Trash or Treasure

Make a list of all the things you'd like to buy and keep it with you when you go to garage sales. It's easy to forget what you're looking for when you're pawing through piles on a table. Having a list with you can minimize the time you spend doing so and eliminate the chances of your coming home with things you really don't need.

Downsides to Garage Sale Shopping

It's pretty hard to beat the thrill of finding a treasure and paying next-to-nothing for it, which makes shopping at garage sales so much fun. But garage sale hunting doesn't always result in positive outcomes. Items can break the second you get them home, or you might notice a condition problem you didn't see when you bought the piece. Unlike buying retail, you're stuck with the problem.

Garage sales are very much a caveat emptor experience. Some sellers might try to conceal condition problems, but more often than not they just go unnoticed unless you spend a lot of time scrutinizing the things you want to buy and have the tools you need to do so (for more on this as well as other tips for getting the best deals, turn to Chapter 9).

As a buyer, you have to know what you're doing and what to look for to get the best results from your efforts. If an item you bought turns out to be damaged, broken, or just not what you thought it was, you can't take it back and ask for a refund. (Well, you could, but it's definitely bad form to do so.) What you can do, however, is put up with it, fix it, toss it, or sell it to someone else—maybe even at your next garage sale!

The Least You Need to Know

- Garage sales—holding them and shopping at them—are one of America's favorite pastimes.

- In addition to being great places for finding bargains, garage sales facilitate the recycling of used items that still have some life to them.

- Garage sales have their good and bad sides. Knowing what the downsides are and addressing potential problems related to them before a sale are the best ways to avoid them.

Goodies vs. Garbage

In This Chapter

- Knowing what to sell
- Knowing what not to sell
- Knowing what to buy
- Knowing what not to buy

All garage sales have two basic elements: items being sold by a seller or sellers and buyers who want to buy those items. These are the ground rules. From here, just about anything goes. Although used household goods and clothing definitely lead the way when it comes to most popular garage sale items, they're by no means the only things that sellers sell and buyers buy. New merchandise, antiques, works of art, collectibles—even foodstuffs are offered at some sales.

The list of things that comprise the sale tables at garage sales is virtually endless. Here's how to know how to separate the goodies from the garbage, regardless of what side of the table you're on.

What to Sell

How do you know which items you should sell at your garage sale and which items should just go into the garbage can? Here's the basic philosophy: Just about everything has some value to it. Maybe the value of some things isn't very high in your eyes, but that doesn't mean that they're not worth something to someone else.

Not convinced yet? Here's a list of objects that people routinely throw away thinking that they're not worth anything. But they are worth something, even if it's just a few cents, and they'll sell at a garage sale:

- **Margarine tubs with lids.** Not only are they good for storing leftovers, they can also be used as reservoirs for watering plants like African violets.

- **Old canning jars without lids.** They might not be acceptable for canning purposes, but they're great for just about anything else you want to do with them.

- **Torn jeans.** Even if they're ripped to shreds, chances are they'll yield enough fabric for patching someone else's jeans.

- **A couple tiles left over from repairing the bathroom wall.** Fit each bottom corner with one of those round rubber glass protectors, and voilà! Instant kitchen trivet or soft-drink coaster.

- **The stub ends of burnt candles.** Crafters melt them down to make new ones.

- **Old T-shirts.** They make great polishing cloths.

Get the idea? Even the things that you think are virtually worthless can be grist for the garage sale mill. With some exceptions, which you'll read about later in this chapter, you really can sell just about everything at your garage sale, which also means you'll be cutting down on what you throw away and on your contribution to your local landfill as well.

Insider Information

When I first attacked my house looking for items to sell, I thought it would be silly and embarrassing to put some of these things out for sale. But, after many years of experience, I learned one important fact: Everything has worth to someone out there. Don't throw anything away! One person's junk is definitely another person's treasure.

—Cathy Pedigo

Here are even more items that you may never have considered selling:

- **Cosmetics.** The makeup mistakes you've made don't have to linger in a drawer where you're reminded of your shopping blunder every time you see them. Clean them up if you've used them, price them right, and they'll sell. Don't forget half-used bottles of nail polish or half-full bottles of perfume, either. Just because you're tired of a color or a scent doesn't mean there isn't a buyer for them.

- **Hair products.** Last year's sparkly pomade might be old news to you, but there will definitely be a kid or a teen out there who will be thrilled to pick up a pot or a tube of the stuff at a bargain. Your daughter no longer needs her collection of barrettes and hair bands now that she's wearing her hair in a Mohawk? Sell them.

- **Underwear.** Yes, this gets into the ooky category for lots of people, but both used and new items will sell.

- **Unfinished craft projects.** Didn't get around to making those gel candles for holiday gifts last year? Don't think you'll ever finish that huge hooked rug that you've been working on for years? Get rid of the guilty feeling you get every time you walk past the cupboard where you've stored the materials and sell them at your next garage sale.

If you're still on the fence about this all-inclusive approach, spend some time going to other sales in your area. Look to see what other sellers are offering for sale as well as what people are buying. While you're at the sales, also notice how merchandise is being sold, how it's being displayed and what the prices are.

You'll find lots of tips on finding things to sell in the next chapter. For now, keep in mind that virtually everything you own can be sold at a garage sale. So quit throwing things away!

Ka-Ching!

Don't get rid of broken items such as can openers, toasters, TVs, lawn mowers, computers, and stereos. People who love to tinker will buy these items at low prices in hopes that they can fix them.

What Not to Sell

With so many things being fair game for selling at a garage sale, there really aren't many items that you shouldn't or can't sell. However, there are some products that you should definitely think twice about before selling for various reasons, and some things that you'd be breaking the law if you sold. For example, it's illegal to resell prescription drugs of any type. Some municipalities ban the sale of new items, items owned by other individuals, or food at garage sales held in their jurisdiction (for more on this, turn to Chapter 4).

Antiques

It's every garage sale shopper's dream to happen across a rare and priceless antique offered for sale by a hapless seller who didn't know better. Don't let that hapless seller be you. Garage sales are not the places to sell antiques unless you don't mind selling them for considerably less than what they're worth. People are not coming to a garage sale to pay big bucks for valuables like these.

If you have any questions about what certain belongings are worth, have them appraised by a licensed appraiser. If you want to sell them, look for an antiques shop that will buy them or take them on consignment for you. Another option is to sell them at an online auction site such as eBay.

Fine and Costume Jewelry

Most people recognize the value in a gold ring or a diamond-encrusted watch, but when it comes to pieces made with pearls and semi-precious stones, value is sometimes more difficult to discern. For this reason, the same caution given for antiques also applies to jewelry. Have any pieces that you think might be worth something appraised before you sell them. What you think is nothing more than costume jewelry might be worth far more than what you'd sell it for at a garage sale.

Insider Information

I bought a set of pearls at a yard sale for 10 cents, thinking my daughter who makes crafts out of junk jewelry could use them. It turns out what I bought was a genuine strand of white pearls with an inset pearl clasp. I wear them almost daily now and the insurance company had them appraised at $3,000! It just goes to show you can never judge a book by its cover.
—J. D.

Some costume jewelry is also valuable enough to make it worth selling at other venues than garage sales. If you want to sell it at your sale, consult a good price guide or research selling prices at online auction sites and price your pieces accordingly. Avid collectors know what the going prices are, and will pay them, although they'd much rather buy these items for a song. Again, don't let it be your song that they're singing unless you are more interested in getting rid of things than making good money while doing so.

Hazardous Products

Baby-related products comprise the largest area of concern when it comes to hazardous items. If they've been stored away for years they may have been manufactured before product safety standards were put into effect and are probably not up to current industry standards. A number of products—baby-related and not—have also been recalled in recent years. The following list, gleaned from the Consumer Product Safety Division's website, details items that you should destroy rather than sell due to the hazards they present:

- **Portable outdoor heaters that don't have oxygen depletion sensors.** The sensor monitors falling oxygen levels and shuts off the heater before it can produce serious levels of carbon monoxide.

- **Soft or loose bedding for babies.** Nonfitted sheets, comforters, sheepskin, and pillows can mold around a child's face and cause suffocation or strangulation.

- **Power strips or extension cords that don't have UL or ETL certification labels.** Products lacking these labels may not be able to handle adequate levels of electrical current and could result in fires. Also avoid these products if they don't have polarized plugs; i.e., plugs that have one blade slightly wider than the other.

- **Hair dryers with plain plugs.** Many dryers manufactured before 1991 won't protect the user from electrocution if the product is dropped into the water. If the dryer has a large, box-shape plug, called a Ground Fault Circuit Interrupter, you're good to go. If it doesn't, destroy it.

- **Old Halloween costumes.** Many costumes were made before the Flammable Fabrics Act was passed, which requires manufacturers to use nonflammable fabrics when making these products. If a costume was made since the act was passed, it will have a label stating that it is flame resistant.

- **Old cribs.** These items may have lots of character, but they're also huge safety hazards. Never sell a crib that has cutout designs on the headboard or footboard or that has slats spaced wider than $2\frac{3}{8}$ inches (about the width of a soda can). Other hazards to watch for are cribs with posts that extend more than $\frac{1}{16}$ inch above the end panel, loose or missing hardware, and cracked or peeling paint.

- **Accordion-style baby gates.** Manufactured before February 1985, these gates have large V-shape openings along the top edge and diamond-shape openings below. Both can entrap a child's head and cause suffocation or strangulation.

- **Toy chests without spring-loaded supports to hold the lids open.** The lids on these chests can fall on a child's head or neck or suffocate a child trapped inside. If you want to sell a chest like this, install a spring-loaded support that will hold the lid up. Or take the lid off.

- **Children's clothing with hood or neckline drawstrings.** These can strangle children if they get caught on playground equipment, a crib, a fence, an escalator, even school buses. You can sell them if you remove the drawstrings on hoods or around the neck, and cut the drawstrings at the waist or bottom of jackets and sweatshirts to three inches.

- **Zippered beanbag chairs.** Not only can children crawl inside them and suffocate, they can also choke on the loose beans or foam pellets used to fill many of these products.

If you don't think an item is safe enough for your own family, don't sell it. It's always better to be safe than sorry, and the last thing you want to do is pass along a safety hazard to another family. If you have concerns about a particular product, check the Consumer Product Safety Center's website at www. cpsc.gov, which has up-to-date information on hazardous items and products that have been recalled.

Items with Deep Sentimental Value

Although it's highly commendable and honorable to sweep your home clean of clutter and unwanted items, there are times when it makes some sense to hang on to certain things. If you're undecided about selling objects that you have an emotional or sentimental attachment to, definitely think twice about including them in your sale. You might feel differently about them the next time you plan a sale, in which case you can include them then.

Trash or Treasure

If you're having second thoughts about selling some items because of the sentiments attached to them, try the "out of sight, out of mind" approach and pack them away until the next time you have a sale. You might find that you're less attached to them than you thought you were by the time your sale rolls around.

Knowing What to Buy

Garage and yard sales are classic venues for young families and other bargain hunters looking for inexpensive items to furnish their homes or for clothing to meet the needs of growing families. They're also great places for finding items of a personal nature, such as clothing, hair dryers, massagers, and the like. Collectors also regularly mine garage sales for items to add to their collections, as well as for

items to sell to other collectors. The chances are
good of your finding just about everything you want
or need if you make the rounds of the sales often
enough. What you want to avoid, however, is paying
too much for what you buy.

Household Goods

If you're shopping for household goods, most of the
items you're going to be interested in aren't considered collectibles or antiques, so price guides that cover
these categories are generally not of much help.

What will help you determine fair pricing is going
around to some garage sales before you start buying.
Keep an eye on what's being sold and for how much.
Also watch what's being bought to get an idea of the
objects that are most in demand.

Trash or Treasure

Many pieces of furniture and household
fixtures from the 1950s and 1960s are now
highly collectible and are becoming increas-
ingly more difficult to find. Set your sights
on items from the 1970s on, and you'll
have better luck finding what you need.

Crock Pots, for example, fell out of favor after their
heyday in the 1970s and 1980s, and you almost couldn't
give them away for a while. However, there's been a
resurgence in their popularity over the past five years
or so, and their numbers at garage sales are dropping.

Here are some other household items that you may or may not be able to find at garage sales depending on where they are in their popularity swings:

- **Fondue pots.** Another very popular item to give newlyweds back in the 1970s; they're now being discovered by a whole new generation. Used fondue sets sometimes turn up but they're somewhat scarce these days.

- **Ice-cream freezers.** The old-fashioned types that you load with salt and crank the handles on tend to show up at sales when the seller has upgraded to models that are easier and faster.

- **Bread machines.** These are becoming more available as many people who bought them thinking they were such a great idea didn't use them as much as they thought they would and are tired of devoting precious counter space to them.

- **Sleeper sofas.** Heavy and clunky, most people would rather sell them than move them. Even thrift shops don't like taking sleeper sofas because they're so hard to move, so you will see them at garage sales.

- **Futons.** Many young couples sell their old ones when they upgrade to beds with mattresses and box springs.

- **Iron skillets.** Some people swear by them. Enough people do, in fact, to make them somewhat scarce at garage sales these days. Certain types of skillets are collectible.

- **Waffle irons.** These are also becoming more scarce as more people try to take time out of their busy schedules to focus on some of life's little pleasures.

- **Electric deep-fryers.** You'll probably see more of them now that some studies have linked fried potatoes to elevated cancer risks.

- **Pyrex mixing bowls.** Certain patterns and colors are becoming very collectible, which makes them more scarce at garage sales.

Other household goods that are perennial "best buys" at garage sales include picture frames, clocks, dishes, silverware, cooking utensils, and small kitchen appliances such as can openers, toasters, microwaves, and toaster ovens. Larger goods that can be found at some sales include sofas, coffee tables, dining room sets, lamps, bedroom sets, and other pieces of furniture. You might have to look past layers of paint and flocked upholstery, but they're worth buying if they're sound pieces in every other way but cosmetically, or if they have minor problems that can easily be fixed.

Think twice about buying any product that has been recalled (see the list discussed earlier in this chapter), although you might consider buying them (and destroying them when you get them home) to make sure they won't harm anyone else.

Other items to avoid buying at garage sales include the following:

- Pesticides and other hazardous chemicals, especially if they're not in their original containers.

- Other potentially dangerous items, such as rickety ladders and old space heaters that lack carbon monoxide detection devices.

Although sellers shouldn't offer potentially dangerous goods, it does happen, either through ignorance or greed. Remember the garage sale credo—buyer beware. You alone are the best protection against buying products that can injure you or others.

If you're a collector, you probably already know if garage sales are good venues for finding the items you're after. If you're new to this pursuit, get a good, up-to-date price guide and research it thoroughly so you'll be able to recognize good pieces and prices on the spot. Also read up on your collecting categories to learn what to look for, such as marks, patterns and colors, as well as condition changes that affect value. You'll find some resources for both in Appendix B.

 Insider Information _____

My sister was in need of a dining table when she happened onto one at a yard sale. It was covered in thick white paint with pits and scratches in it. She paid $20. She took it home, stripped the paint off it and revarnished it. Beneath the paint was a lovely table with carved legs and designs carved into the sides. A lady came to visit and offered to buy the refinished table for $800.

—Anonymous, Douglasville, Georgia

Another good way to get the feel for garage sale prices is to check what's being bought and sold at online auctions. However, you should use these prices only as guidelines. Two of the key reasons people sell online are the ability to have their items viewed by many more people than would see them at a garage sale, and the potential for selling them at higher prices than they would locally.

Clothing and Accessories

If you know anything at all about garage sales, you know they can be great places for picking up children's clothing for a song, and for finding gently worn and even new pieces for adults as well. However, garage sales can also be treasure troves for finding items that look like they just came off the runway. Here's why: Nothing is ever really new in the fashion industry, which means that styles that were in vogue at some point in the past always come back. For spring and fall 2002, wide leather belts were the big story. They were in the 1960s, too. The boots that were made for walking in the 1970s are just as popular today as they were 30 years ago.

Although many of the high demand pieces from yesteryear have already been bought up—some of them many years ago—garage sales can still yield clothing that's old but not quite vintage, such as bellbottom pants and fringed vests from the 1960s, and long scarves, crocheted ponchos and Frye boots from the 1970s. You might even find pieces that date back to before the 1960s, such as beaded sweaters and circle skirts from the 1950s.

> **Trash or Treasure**
>
> Fit is often an issue with older clothing as people were smaller than they are today. Old pieces can also be somewhat misleading and look bigger than they actually are. You might be able to alter some pieces. If not, you can try to make them into something else.

Other items to look for in this category include:

- **Old tennis shoes,** especially Converse, certain types of Keds, Vans, etc. Adidas from the early 1970s are collectible, especially if they're in good condition.

- **Beaded items,** such as necklaces and earrings. Beads were very popular during the flapper years of the 1920s, and you may find long beaded ropes with tassels from that period that were used as belts and necklaces. They were also popular during the hippie years of the 1960s, and pieces from this era also occasionally show up at garage sales.

- **Costume jewelry.** If you read the earlier part of this chapter, you already saw the advice we gave about having these items appraised if they seem to have value. However, most sellers won't bother to go to the trouble or expense of doing so, and they especially won't do it if the items are in need of repair; i.e., lacking some stones, bent in spots, corroded, enameling wearing off, etc. This means you'll get some great deals on signed pieces from

the 1930s, 1940s, 1950s, 1960s, and 1970s if
you know what you're looking for.

- **Purses.** Old purses—those dating back to
  the 1930s and earlier—have been collectible
  for a long time, and they rarely show up at
  garage sales. What you might see, however,
  are the new collectibles—older purses by
  Coach, Etienne Aigner and Gucci; tooled,
  Western-style leather bags from the 1940s on;
  alligator purses of any vintage, and so on.

As much as you might like a particular article of
clothing, steer clear if it has more than just light
staining on any part, and especially under the arms.
Set-in stains rarely come out completely, although
you'd be amazed at what a little lemon juice or
vinegar can do. Also reject items that smell funky.
A good airing or dry-cleaning might get rid of body
odor or the smell left over from storing pieces in
cedar chests or mothballs for extended periods of
time. Then again, it might not.

Costume jewelry can be problematic to repair if
broken, although these pieces are worth buying if
you can use their components, such as rhinestones,
to repair other items. Pieces made of sterling silver
can often be soldered. It's also no big deal to glue
on missing pin backs or earring backs, so don't
immediately reject pieces that are missing them.

Personal Items

Some people find the thought of buying personal
items—toiletries, personal appliances, cosmetics,

and the like—at a garage sale too squeamish for words. Others will buy almost anything if the price is right. If you're somewhere in the middle, let your gut feelings and some common sense guide you when shopping in this category.

Many personal products sold at garage sales are new and never used. They might be on the sales table because the purchaser bought the wrong thing and didn't return it in time, or the sale was final and the item couldn't be returned. Most makeup and perfume sold definitely falls into this category, or they might be items from "gift with purchase" or "purchase with purchase" packages that the seller had no use for or didn't like. If you're at a sale where lots of sample sizes are being sold, it's a pretty good bet that the seller buys makeup on a fairly regular basis, so the samples are probably pretty fresh.

 Insider Information

I went to a huge "we're moving, everything must go" sale. There was tons of stuff, including an unused package of Today Sponges (the ultimate in feminine contraception!). It has been hot here and they were sitting out in the sun. Unless it's a Planned Parenthood Rummage Sale, I will continue to refuse to buy my birth control at yard sales!

—T., Los Angeles

It goes without saying that you should avoid buying anything that's clearly seen better days or that doesn't appear to be sanitary. However, if other items being sold look to be in good shape and of good quality, you can assume that any personal products being sold are of similar quality. Although there are definitely exceptions to this, most sellers won't put out items that they're embarrassed to sell.

Products like nail polish and nonaerosol hair styling aids are almost always safe to buy as there's not much beyond improper storage that can alter their properties. About the worst that can happen is that they'll thicken or separate, and it's pretty easy to fix both problems. It's a little trickier when it comes to perfume and makeup. If the product appears brand new, or is close to it, the chances of it being contaminated or spoiled are lower than if it's half gone. However, cosmetics and fragrances also have shelf lives, which means that a full bottle of foundation that was only used once or twice might have degraded because it's been around too long. Fragrances that are old or improperly stored will become less intense or actually go bad just like wine does.

In general, it's a good idea to avoid any product or device that looks questionable or smells a little off. Other personal items that can send up warning flags include the following:

- **Expired over-the-counter drugs.** Also pass up any over-the-counter drugs in boxes with stained corners (signs of potential water damage) or that don't have expiration dates at all, which means they were manufactured before it was common to date such products.

- **Mascara.** Also think twice about other cosmetics that are used around the eyes as they can be easily contaminated.

- **Hair coloring products.** Improper storage in conditions that are too cold or too hot can alter their properties. Definitely pass them by if they're past their expiration date.

Also pass up any personal care appliances, such as facial steamers, electric manicure sets, hot rollers and the like if they don't have up-to-date cords and plugs. Think twice about buying them if their plugs are up to date but the cords are frayed. This signifies hard use, and most personal care appliances aren't made to last forever. The amount of time and money you spend repairing them isn't worth the effort when the heater coil or motor dies on you a month later.

The Least You Need to Know

- With just a few exceptions, you can sell almost anything at a garage sale.

- Steer clear of selling (or buying) any potentially hazardous products.

- Let your common sense and gut feelings guide you when buying personal items at a garage sale.

3

Gathering Your Inventory

In This Chapter

- Thinking like a retailer
- Pillaging your parlor
- Increasing your inventory
- Storing your stuff

As you read in Chapter 2, you can sell just about anything at a garage sale—old margarine tubs, the burnt-down ends of used candles—you name it. Those odds and ends, the bits and pieces you thought weren't worth very much, can add up to big money. But only if you have enough of them.

The concept of the table of plenty definitely applies to garage sales. Not only can you sell just about anything, you want to have lots to sell. Full sales tables and packed clothes racks are like magnets to buyers. The more things you have for them to browse through, the longer they'll stay and the more money they'll spend. Stock your garage sale like retailers stock their stores, and you're guaranteed big profits.

Thinking Like a Retailer

When you have a home-based sale—garage, yard, porch, attic, what have you—you're a seller offering goods to buyers who want to buy them. Looking at it another way, you're basically becoming a specialty retailer for the length of time you have your sale. Unlike other retailers, however, you're selling used goods (unless you're living in an area that permits selling new items at garage sales). You're not giving your belongings away, you're not bartering them for products or services. You're offering them for sale, and people are paying for them with cold hard cash.

When you start thinking like a retailer, all the hard work that goes into a garage sale starts to make more sense. If you're after big money, you want to do everything you can to maximize your sales. You want to make sure that you're offering merchandise that people want, and you're going to execute a marketing plan to make sure that people know you have them. You're going to price your things right, you're going to display them attractively, and you're going to provide your buyers with a comfortable place to shop.

You'll read more about how to do all of this in the chapters ahead. At this point, however, your challenge is to make sure you have enough inventory on hand so your garage sale will be a success. Wondering where it's all going to come from? Don't think you have enough to sell? Chances are very good that you're surrounded by a treasure trove of inventory. You just haven't discovered it yet.

Diving for Dollars

You might have already gone through your house and gathered up everything you thought you could sell. But did you do it systemically? Did you go through every room with a fine-tooth comb? Were you ruthless about attacking closets and drawers? Did you dive under beds and climb into crawl spaces? If not, you're going to be amazed at how much more you can find to sell.

We'll be honest—most people don't enjoy the inventory gathering part of garage sales. It's especially hard to do if you or your family members tend to be pack rats, as getting rid of things goes against your nature. If it's your first sale, the amount of stuff you find can be overwhelming. But remember your main goal—to make money. If you can stay focused on this goal, the gathering process will be easier.

Trash or Treasure

Protect against seller's remorse by putting items into boxes with lids or black plastic bags the second you decide to sell them. Out of sight, out of mind!

If you're still having trouble with the thought of selling your possessions, it might help to remember the words of that great minimalist Henry David Thoreau: "Most of the luxuries, and many of the so-called comforts of life, are not only dispensable, but positive hindrances to the elevation of humanity."

Attacking Your House

The first step is to gather up everything you can sell by going through every inch of your house. You're going to take various home items captive, one room at a time, one day at a time, at your own pace. It doesn't matter what order you go in. What does matter is that you're thorough and you leave no stone unturned, no corner unchecked, no drawer undumped.

If this is the first time you've had a garage sale, the gathering process is going to take you some time. You can approach the time factor in one of two ways: start months ahead of your planned sales date to ensure that you are done collecting your inventory in time, or tell yourself that you will sell everything you can gather within a certain time period, say a week or 20 hours, whatever works for you. Keep in mind that it's better to have smaller sales more frequently than one mega-sale every 5 or 10 years or so. Not only are smaller sales easier to manage, the merchandise you sell at them will be fresher, more up to date, and most likely more desirable to a larger number of buyers.

Arm yourself with some large black trash bags or paper grocery bags for soft and unbreakable items, and some boxes, preferably with lids or tops, for breakables. Also have on hand the following items:

- A marking pen for labeling the contents of boxes.

- Masking tape, for marking the contents of bags.

- Labels or other price tags. You don't have to price items as you gather them, but it will save you time later if you do. See Chapter 7 for suggestions on the various materials you can use for pricing your goods.

You can clean your inventory later, but it's often easier to dust things off and polish them up while you're gathering them together. If you decide to do it now, stick some cleaning products in one of your boxes. But don't knock yourself out on cleaning. Spiffing up that old toaster might bring in a few extra bucks. Dishes, glasses and silverware will always benefit from a good cleaning in the dishwasher. Clothing should always be freshly laundered and pressed. However, it's not worth your time and effort to make everything you're selling—especially stuff that's worth a quarter or two at best—look like it's brand new. Sometimes a lick and a promise is enough.

Capturing Your Kitchen

Begin your search in that dark cavern under your kitchen sink. You'll be surprised at what you'll find there. Didn't like the way that dishwasher detergent smelled? Sell it! The drain stopper that no longer fits your new sink? Add it to your pile. Rubber gloves that were too big for you? Put them in the sale.

Look through every kitchen drawer, including the one under your oven. Search your cabinets, pantry, shelves, closets, etc. Examine each and every item in these places. Determine how long it's been since you used them and if you even need them. Toss everything you don't want into your bags and boxes. Make it a challenge to see how much you can collect just from that first room.

Trash or Treasure

If you store the plastic bags from your grocery store under the sink, take them all out and stick them into a larger bag—the spot where they were will fill up like magic and you can use the old ones to bag up merchandise at your garage sale.

Garage sales are great for getting rid of small appliances, such as toasters, can openers, toaster ovens, etc., that you no longer use or want to replace. If you're tired of your cookware or silverware and you want to get something new, sell it. If items don't sell, just stick them back in your kitchen after your sale and try them again the next time. If they do sell, then you get to go pick out shiny new things.

Blasting Through the Bathroom

Open up your medicine cabinet and inspect each item. Grab any unused over-the-counter medicines you decided you didn't like or can't use for some reason (make sure they're not past their expiration dates, though). Believe it or not, somebody else would love to have these items for a discounted price.

Look under the sinks and inside any closets. Collect soaps, toiletries, brushes that aren't used anymore, hair items, old towels, your own hamper—they will sell! Are you getting tired of that old toilet seat cover and matching rug? Grab them and add them to your pile. If they sell, you can go out and buy yourself a new set. If they don't, just put them back on and hope they sell at your next sale.

Mastering the Master Bedroom

Again, as you enter this room, be in attack mode. Go through every drawer, closet, nook, and cranny. If you store things under the bed, drag out those boxes. Don't forget things like the following:

- Old underwear
- Half bottles of perfume you decided you didn't like
- Makeup products that you never used or are half used
- Clothes, hats, gloves, and scarves
- Trinkets, knick-knacks, and jewelry
- Pillows and baskets

All of it can be a great find for someone else and a gold mine for you.

Corralling Your Kids' Rooms

If your kids are old enough to understand that you want to sell some of their possessions, it's definitely a good idea to enlist their help and make this stage of the war a mutual attack. It usually isn't much of a battle to get children to part with clothing, but when it comes to stuffed animals and toys it's easy to start a mini-riot. It's amazing how a little one can suddenly become very interested in a cast-off doll or Teddy bear the second you mention the possibility of selling it.

Even if your children are away at school, ask their permission before selling their stuff. Things that may top your list as perfect fodder for a garage sale could be priceless to them, and might be worth more than you think, especially if they've become the hot new collectibles.

Trash or Treasure

Many parents get their kids on the garage sale bandwagon by telling them that getting rid of old toys helps make space for new ones. You can even take this a step further by teaching your children the value of a buck. Do this by letting them have a mini garage sale while your sale is going on. Help them price their stuff, and set them up at their own table. At the end of the day, the proceeds from their sales can be theirs to keep.

Talk to your children about why you want to get rid of some of their belongings. Tell them that getting rid of old things makes room for new things. Also talk to them about what will happen to items that don't sell. Tell them that you're going to donate their old clothes and unsold toys to charity (if that's what you're planning to do) so that other children will have things to play with and clothing to wear.

First put aside anything you might want to save as hand-me-downs, and then begin the hunt. Make it fun. Send your kids on seek and find missions. Toss the things they come back with into a bag as soon as you get your hands on them. Wait until later to tag or clean them—the sooner you get items out of sight, the sooner they're forgotten.

Things to throw into the kiddie pile include the following:

- Stuffed animals, dolls, and toys
- Skates
- Games
- Coloring books, workbooks, and storybooks the kids have outgrown
- Crayons, markers, chalk, scissors, and other craft items
- Old clothing, including socks, shoes, underwear, pajamas, robes, pants, shirts, belts, etc.

Don't throw away those old socks, underwear, or torn jeans. All of it will sell.

Clearing the Linen Closet

There might be a gold mine of things you've forgotten about stored in the linen closet. Gather up tablecloths, sheets, linens, towels, bedspreads, mattress pads, and cleaning supplies that you don't want anymore. Even torn sheets and tattered blankets will sell if you price them right. People always need soft towels and cloths for polishing or cleaning delicate items. Bags of them sell for $3 to $4 at big-box retailers and hardware stores. Stuff the ones you have that are tattered beyond use into one of your plastic bags and sell the bag for $1.

Ravaging the Living Room

Look inside of end tables, coffee tables, desks, and every nook and cranny in your living room. You might find old magazines, records, tapes, CDs, books, pictures, gadgets, old lamps, and electronic equipment—and it's all fodder for your garage sale.

Launching Into the Laundry Room

Laundry rooms are not only good sources for cleaning items you no longer need, they also tend to be repositories for other cast-offs, such as clothing that needs mending, shoes that need resoling, and other household items that have become displaced from their usual locations for some reason or another. If these items have been sitting on the counters or in the cupboards of your laundry room for a while, chances are pretty good that they're no longer needed. Add them to your inventory.

Conquering Crawl Space, Basements, Attics, and Garages

It can take courage to attack the crawl spaces, basements, attics, and garages. When you do, don't be surprised if your efforts take awhile, especially if you've been throwing unused and unwanted items into these places for some time. The things you find stashed away in these areas will most likely be in various states of repair or disrepair. Don't be selective. Include it all, even broken items. Even if things seem useless to you, they might not to others.

Some of the things you'll find in these spots are obvious garage sale goodies, such as furniture, pictures, vases, appliances, bicycles (rusty or not), humidifiers, lawnmowers—the list is virtually endless.

Ka-Ching!

Don't overlook other potential inventory items such as old building or landscaping materials. Lots of buyers are looking for found objects for any number of reasons. Sometimes they're not even looking for specific items, but they'll buy them when they see them. The scrap lumber you had left over from building your basement workbench might be just enough for a beading enthusiast to construct a loom from. Don't take a chance on missing a sale because you didn't include things that you felt had dubious value. Take a chance on it all.

Other Rooms to Conquer

If you have a home office, craft room, or sewing room, don't leave them off your attack list. They're all potential gold mines for boosting your garage sale inventory. Old computer software, abandoned craft projects, the electric pencil sharpener you got one year as a present and never used, even that half-full box of bulletin board push pins—add them all to your sale pile.

Increasing Your Inventory

Okay, so you've attacked your house. You've been merciless. You've gathered up everything you can possibly put your hands on, and you still don't have enough to make your garage sale look fully stocked. Time to cancel your plans? Absolutely not. There are lots of ways to increase your inventory. You just have to expand your circle of exploration, and maybe get a little creative about it. Some methods are free. With others, you'll have to pay a little to get a little.

Other Garage Sales

If you needed another reason to shop at other garage sales, here it is. Most people who have garage sales significantly underprice the things they sell at them. When you go to sales where you can buy stuff for a song, scoop it up, re-price it, and sell it at your own sale.

Don't for a minute think that there's anything wrong or immoral about doing this. You're not taking advantage of the previous owners. If you hadn't bought their goods, someone else would have. It's not your fault that the sellers decided to sell their things for less than what they were worth. You're doing nothing different from what antiques and flea market dealers do—you're finding sellable merchandise, paying good prices for it, offering others good deals on it, and making a profit while doing it.

However, there's a difference between picking up a few items to flesh out an occasional garage sale and buying enough merchandise to stock an ongoing retail business that you operate out of your home under the guise of a yard or garage sale. Before you do any of this, check your local laws. See what's on the books regarding both the sale of new merchandise at garage sales and how occasional sales—the category in which garage and yard sales fall into—are regulated and taxed.

As you'll read more about in Chapter 4, ordinances, laws, and regulations regarding garage and yard sales can vary greatly. Some municipalities will let you sell new merchandise along with old; others prohibit it. Some will let you sell new merchandise if you register as a retail business. This raises the level of scrutiny on your sales, and also makes you liable for paying sales taxes if they're collected where you live, and for claiming your sales as income on your tax returns.

> ### Insider Information
>
> One summer I was able to purchase several hundred old romance paperbacks for only one cent each at another person's garage sale. I had a fun winter reading them, and then I sold them the next summer for a huge profit—20 cents each—for a profit of $57!
>
> —Cathy Pedigo

Closeouts and Markdowns

If you live in an area that will let you sell new merchandise at your garage sale, keep an eye out for merchandise closeouts and markdowns when shopping at your favorite stores. If you're in the right place at the right time (right after the holidays when retailers are frantically clearing their shelves of excess inventory to make way for new merchandise is one of them), you can run across some fabulous clearances, such as $20 items marked down to $1.69. When that happens, buy all they have (or as much as you can afford) and stash it away.

If it's really good merchandise, use some of your stash for presents during the year, and sell what you have left at your next sale. If you happen to stumble upon a really good deal, but it's too much for your budget, see if you can find a friend or relative to go in on it with you.

Going-out-of-business and store or merchandise liquidation sales are other possible sources for garage sale goods. If the sellers are serious about getting rid of their stuff, you should be able to buy it for a fraction of its value.

Dollar Stores

Most of the stuff at dollar stores isn't worth much more than what you pay for it, but they can be good resources for finding little cheap items—things like hair combs, barrettes, kitchen scrubbies, and the like—to round out your inventory if you're in short supply of such goods.

Ka-Ching!

Dollar store merchandise is often packaged in multiples. You might be able to break the packages apart and sell the individual items for more than what you paid for the pack.

Thrift Shops

There usually aren't many bargains to be had at thrift shops as most merchandise is priced high enough to return a profit to the shop. However, many thrift shops hold special sales at various times of the year so they can clear their shelves of old merchandise and make room for new goods. Check with your local shops to see when their sales are scheduled. You might have to paw through lots of stuff, but chances are pretty good that you'll find some things that you can mark up and sell.

Trash or Treasure

As a general rule, don't buy anything for reselling at your garage sale unless you think you can sell it for at least twice what you paid for it.

If you're on vacation and there are some interesting looking thrift shops near by, think about looking for garage sale merchandise at them if you have some spare time. You might find some good prices on things that cost a little more at home as well as items that might be in short supply where you live.

Coupons and Refunds

If you're the thrifty type who cuts coupons, watches for sales, and mails in rebate slips, add the fruits of your labor to your garage sale inventory. Lotions, shampoos, deodorants, cleaning products—even sample sizes of these products sell.

Dumpster Diving

Dumpster diving is definitely not for the squeamish, but going through other people's garbage can yield some great garage sale merchandise. Be careful if you're going to try this. In some areas, garbage picking is against the law. Even if it isn't, Dumpster diving can be risky business as it's amazingly easy to injure yourself on broken glass and other damaged items. And be prepared for some embarrassment if you get caught doing it.

Friends and Family

If you have friends of family members who need to declutter their homes but either don't like to have garage sales or don't have the time to organize their own, see if they would like you to take their castoffs off their hands for them. If they hem and haw a bit, or tell you that they're hanging on to their things in anticipation of their own sale sometime in the future, you can sweeten the deal (worth it if they have good stuff that you're itching to get your hands on) by offering to split the proceeds from the sale of their items, take them on consignment, or buy them outright.

Insider Information _____

After I saw how many people regularly cruised the alley behind my house looking for treasures in the trash, I started doing it myself and was amazed at what I found—chairs in need of some TLC, books and magazines, even perfectly good kitchen items that people decided they didn't want for some reason. My best find were two Dumpsters full of construction materials, new and used items from two duplexes being renovated just down the block. I called a friend and hauled away two carloads of bricks, wood, shutters, vintage tiles, even bathroom and light fixtures. I didn't have a place to store it all, so I threw an ad in the paper and had a garage sale that same weekend. It was the best sale I ever had!

—J. J., Minnetonka, Minnesota

Some garage sale pros even run ads in the paper saying they'll buy unwanted goods for garage sales. If you're serious about having garage sales on a regular basis, and you don't have enough of your own inventory to keep things going, this approach might be worth a try. Be sure, though, that you know enough about buying used goods to be able to set fair prices for both the sellers and you.

Drinks and Food

Some municipalities allow the sale of pre-packaged drinks and snack items at garage sales. Check to see if you can sell them where you live. If so, definitely consider adding them to your inventory. Not only is it a nice touch to offer people sustenance while they're shopping with you, they'll stay longer if you do. Watch for sales on canned drinks and snacks throughout the year and stockpile these products when you see them. Most snack items have long enough shelf lives to allow you to do this, but be sure to keep an eye on the expiration dates. It probably isn't much of a risk to sell merchandise that's a little past its prime. Go much beyond that, however, and it's better to be safe than sorry.

If your kids are old enough to handle the responsibility (and know the basics of good hygiene), you can give them a taste of the entrepreneurial spirit and let them set up a lemonade stand. Or let them manage the soft drink and snack sales.

Where to Put Your Inventory

Now that you've amassed all this stuff, where are you going to put it? The best approach is to allocate a part of your basement, attic, garage, or whatever area you choose in your home as your garage sale storage area. This will be the place that you'll run to all year long with your items—outgrown clothes, broken and unwanted items, etc. By the time you have your next garage sale, you'll be amazed at all the things you've collected.

Insider Information _____

I begin to mark prices on stored items approximately one month ahead of my garage sales, so I'm not overwhelmed a week before the sale. Sometimes I mark my items as I store them in their designated area. This really cuts down on all the last minute preparation time before your sale, and I recommend it highly!

—Cathy Pedigo

If you've gathered up more things than you can comfortably store in your home, see if a friend, family member, or neighbor wouldn't mind helping you out by letting you stash some of your stuff off-site. If you have far more merchandise than you know what to do with, check into renting a storage space or an unused garage. If you have to go with this approach, however, consider what you're going to have to pay for storing your items with what you think you can get when you sell them. If it's going to cost you more to hang on to them than you'll make selling them, plan a sale as quickly as you can so you can bring your inventory down to a more manageable level.

The Least You Need to Know

- A big inventory is one of the keys to a successful garage sale. The more you have to sell, the more people will buy.

- Leave no stone unturned when gathering garage sale items in your home. Go through every room, every drawer, and every nook and cranny.

- Don't assume that something's not good enough to sell. It might not have much value to you, but it might for someone else.

- If you're thinking about buying new or used merchandise to increase your inventory, first check the local laws governing garage sales in your area. Some areas prohibit selling anything other than used goods that came from your own household.

Planning Your Sale

In This Chapter

- Being legal
- Picking the best times and dates
- Going it alone vs. doing it with neighbors

Garage sales were often spur of the moment events back in their early days. Folks would drag out a table or two or put down a couple blankets on their lawn, pile them with household items collected at the last minute (and usually not priced), stick up a few signs here and there, and wait for any buyers who might happen past their house.

It's possible to make some money with a spur of the moment sale. Some people actually prefer them as they're pretty easy to put on. But time is a precious commodity these days. Why waste yours on a last-minute event that might not be worth even the small amount of time and effort you put into it?

Spend some time planning your sale and the chances of it being successful will be greatly enhanced.

Basic Considerations

If you've never held a garage sale before, or you've moved to a new city or town since you had your last one, check to see what your local authorities have to say about such events. Each town has governing agencies and authorities that make and enforce certain rules and regulations regarding garage sales. Some jurisdictions require a permit. Many limit the number of sales you can hold in a year and how long you can hold them, as well as the number of signs you can put up and when you have to take them down.

 Insider Information _____

> I once made the mistake of having too many sales in one year. I received a letter informing me to shut down my sale immediately because of our township ordinance, which stated that I could only have two separate weeks of garage sales. I pleaded with our authorities and claimed ignorance, and they let me finish out my sale … but with strict instructions not to do it again!
>
> —Cathy Pedigo

For the most part, local restrictions are fairly commonsense. However, you might be surprised at some of the regulations that are on the books. Here are excerpts from some typical garage sale regulations found on the websites for various municipalities around the United States:

- The City of Fullerton in California permits one sale every six months. No sale can last longer than three consecutive days. Sale items may not be displayed or sold in the public right-of-way, such as on a sidewalk. No sales or displays of items may take place after sundown. Commercial merchandise may not be brought in and sold in addition to personal items. Signs are limited to three per sale, and can't be larger than two square feet in area.

- In Medina, Washington, residents don't need a business license but do have to register the garage sale at City Hall. Two sales can be held per calendar year, with no one sale lasting more than two days. Signs are limited to one directly adjacent to the sale site and three temporary signs located offsite. None can exceed two square feet. Violators can be issued a $47 citation.

- Residents of Liberty, Missouri, can hold two garage sales in a 12-month period with each lasting 3 consecutive days. No goods purchased for resale may be offered for sale, nor can consignment goods be sold. Directional signs may not be placed in the street right-of-way or on utility poles.

- Overland Park, Kansas, regulates craft, sample, and estate sales along with garage sales, and does allow the sale of new goods along with used household goods and property. Only one sign at the location of the sale is allowed. No directional signs are allowed. Residents can have two sales per year, each lasting up to four days. No permit is required.

- In Easthampton, Massachusetts, residents can hold garage sales for no more than two days twice a year. Only used, secondhand, or antiques can be offered. All material to be sold must originate from the property that is the site of the sale (e.g., no consignment goods). Individuals holding garage sales must apply for a permit no less than five days before the sale and pay a $5 fee. Nonprofit or religious societies, charities, associations or corporations aren't required to pay a fee.

- Schaumburg, Illinois, allows its residents to hold garage sales on any two consecutive days from Thursday through Sunday from 9 A.M. to 6 P.M. Only two sales can be held per year, and only personal items can be sold. Items purchased for resale purposes cannot be sold. Balloons, streamers, and other attention-getting devices are prohibited. Sellers can sell canned soft drinks and individually pre-packaged bags of snacks and candy. The sale of glass bottles is prohibited. A permit is required and must be displayed at the place of the sale.

The place to check local regulations is usually the office of code regulations or the code enforcement division in the city or municipality where you live. Almost every city and town has a website where you can also access this information.

Trash or Treasure _____

Most municipalities aren't too heavy-handed about cracking down on garage sales that violate local ordinances as they generally have more important things to worry about. However, not knowing the rules can throw a monkey wrench into your plans after you've done all the work to set up your sale. It can also cause you to lose all those signs you painstakingly placed around town if you put up too many and in the wrong places. Why take a chance? Know the rules before you're sorry.

Best Sale Times

Garage sales are traditionally early riser affairs, with the majority of them starting several hours after the sun comes up and continuing on through the afternoon. If the sales in your area cover these hours, it's generally a good idea to plan yours to do so as well in order to attract the best crowds. However, early starts are not the only way to go. If you're having your sale during the week, starting at 10 A.M. or even later can work as well, especially if later starts are the norm for weekday sales in your area. Starting later might also catch people who can't shop early due to other commitments, or who just can't get out of bed for early morning sales.

Use the other sales in your area (and local regulations, of course) to help you determine the hours for your sale. Check the garage sale ads in your paper to get a feel for the most popular start times. If you can't start as early as the others for some reason, however, don't abandon your plans. If you're offering items that people want to buy, and you do a good job promoting your sale, they'll come regardless of the time. Some will even appreciate the opportunity to shop at a sale where the merchandise isn't already picked over because they arrived too late for the best deals.

Ka-Ching!

If possible, start your sale approximately a half-hour earlier than most of the other sales in your area (this is where doing your homework will really pay off). If they're starting at 8 A.M., plan yours for 7:30. This way, you'll grab the early risers and get them to spend their money at your sale before all the others.

When you end your sale isn't as critical as when you start it. Some people plan open-ended sales and stay open for as long as it makes sense to do so. A better plan, however, is to set a specific ending time. In general, plan to keep your sale going for at least six hours each day you have it. Seven or eight hours are better unless you run out of things to sell. If you end your sale too early in the day, you'll have to contend with people coming up to you (or shouting from their cars) and asking, usually in an extremely incredulous tone, if you're really closing up, even though it's clear that you're doing so.

Best Sale Days

It's also part of the garage sale tradition to hold these events during the weekend, and many areas restrict them to days near or on the weekend—Thursday, Friday, Saturday or Friday, Saturday, Sunday being the most common combinations. If you can only have a two-day sale on the weekend, hold it on Friday and Saturday so you can catch people who can attend a weekday sale as well as those who can't. Sunday has never proven to be a great day for garage sales unless you live in a resort or high-traffic area.

Ka-Ching!

If you're including a lot of guy stuff in your sale—things like tools, clothing, and the like—definitely plan to include a Saturday in your sale so you can catch male shoppers who can't come to weekday sales.

One-Day vs. Multiple-Day Sales

Some people believe you should keep your garage sale going for as long as you're allowed to keep the doors open. Some areas even allow extended sales. The thought of having a sale for more than a couple of days may seem daunting, but longer sales—especially if there's enough inventory to sell and they're advertised correctly (see Chapter 6 for more on this) can generate enough income to make it worth the time and effort it takes to hold these protracted events.

Garage Sale Don'ts

Only hold sales for longer than three days if you have enough inventory to support them. It's not worth your time or trouble to drag things out over a longer period of time if you're going to end up with just a few items on the last days of the sale.

Although it's true that having more garage sales will net you more money, you don't have to hold long drawn-out sales to get a good return on your investment. You're always going to get your best crowds and the most money in your pocket on the first day or two of a sale. After that, the law of diminishing returns usually kicks in. Your enthusiasm for continuing the sale will probably start to wane as well.

Garage Sale Don'ts

Even if you live in an area that doesn't prohibit it, don't have a garage sale that just keeps on going ... and going ... and going. People who have sales that go on for days at a time or for weekend upon weekend aren't really having garage sales, they're operating unlicensed businesses. They also don't fall into the "good neighbor" category.

Choose a sale duration that fits your needs and your other commitments. Don't feel like you have to have an extended sale just because you can, or because your neighbors made so much money when they had theirs. If all you can do is a one-day sale, stick with that. A two-day sale is manageable for most people, and will give you better results. If you have the time and resources to hold a sale for a longer length of time, try it and see if you like it.

Special Timing Considerations

Right after payday, say the first or second day of each month and again around the middle of the month, is one of the most profitable times for a garage sale. People still have money left over from their paychecks and can hardly wait to get out and spend some at their favorite pastime.

Holiday weekends can be dicey when it comes to holding a garage sale. In some parts of the country, everyone leaves town. In others, and especially in tourism areas where there are lots of local events going on, you may attract more shoppers. Again, it's good to see how other people schedule their sales. If there aren't many held over holiday weekends, you might want to think twice before planning yours for them as well.

Best Times of the Year

What's the best time of year for a garage sale? Almost any time, really. If your local regulations will permit it, and you're up to the task, have a springtime sale, a summer sale, and a fall sale. If the winter weather is pleasant where you live, there's no reason not to hold one then as well. Each seasonal sale will bring out a variety of shoppers looking for different things. People who come in the spring are looking for summer clothing and just about anything else related to warm weather. If you live in a cold climate, they'll also come in droves because they're so excited about getting out of the house after a long winter with no garage sales to go to. Shoppers at fall sales will be looking for back to school clothes and winter items.

Throughout most of the United States, the best garage sale weather begins in mid- to late spring and continues through the early and mid-fall. This seven-month period—roughly April through October—is when the majority of garage sales are held. However, there's nothing that says you can't hold a porch, basement or attic sale in the dead of winter if you want. Just be prepared for small crowds, especially if there's snow or heavy rain to contend with.

Going Solo vs. Joint Sales

Holding a garage sale—especially a big, multi-day sale—can be extremely hard work for people who don't have family members or friends who can help out. Placing ads and making signs can also get a little pricey, especially when money is tight. It's not uncommon to spend upward of $75 to $100 for ads and signs, especially when you have to buy materials and make a lot of the latter.

For these reasons, some sellers like the notion of sharing resources and expenses with their neighbors by holding a multi-family or neighborhood garage sale. Some municipalities even support such events by sponsoring citywide garage sales and providing free publicity and trash hauling services to remove unsold and unwanted items after the sales are over.

Is participating in a neighborhood or community-wide event right for you? These sales definitely create lots of word-of-mouth buzz and excitement that can attract big crowds, especially if they've been held for enough years to make them a local tradition. As an example, some 5,000 sellers annually participate in one gigantic yard sale that stretches through parts of three states—Alabama, Kentucky, and Tennessee—and attracts thousands of bargain-hunting tourists (turn to Appendix B for more on this event, billed as the world's longest yard sale). If there's something similar where you live, you might miss out on a great sales opportunity if you didn't participate.

Trash or Treasure

If you're going to participate in a multi-family sale, be sure that everyone is in agreement as to how resources are pooled and allocated. It also helps if the members of the group get along well.

Buyers often like the idea of being able to look at items being offered by lots of sellers at the same time. Other reasons to participate in group garage sales include the following:

- The ability to pool promotional resources, as well as the ability to profit from them.
- The camaraderie of doing something with your neighbors or your community.

- Assistance from local officials. As previously mentioned, many municipalities support group garage sales by promoting them and offering free trash-hauling services at the end of the event.

- Being able to spread the responsibility for sign making and posting and other aspects of setting up garage sales.

If you're short on tables or other display items, you might be able to borrow them from neighbors who have more than they need. If you're long on kids, you can send them over to help neighbors who are short-staffed.

While being able to share resources and expenses can be appealing, there are definitely some downsides to group garage sales. One is pretty significant: Many sellers say they don't make as much during these sales. Why? The competition from other sales is the biggest reason.

Put yourself in your customers' shoes. They might come to your sale and get all excited about something they find. But wait! There's another sale across the street, and more sales beyond that. Maybe they can find something better or cheaper elsewhere at one of the sales they haven't yet visited. So they leave your sale and start hitting the others. Maybe they'll come back to yours. Maybe they won't. The more likely scenario is that they'll get sidetracked and forget where you are. They also might spend all their money elsewhere or tire out and decide they're done for the day before they make it back to your place.

Other drawbacks to group or community sales include the following:

- Loss of control. Most of these events have specific starting and ending times and other constraints that may or may not work well for you. If you're combining items from several families into one mega-sale held in one garage or yard, there might be conflicting opinions over how the sale should be organized, how items should be tagged, who does what, and so on.

- The get-along factor. Personality clashes are commonplace in neighborhood sales, although less so in larger, more organized and well-established community events where the rules and regulations are clearly articulated.

- Greater opportunities for theft and other security problems. Larger crowds create many more opportunities for sticky fingers to latch onto your goods while you're busy helping someone else.

- More looky-loos, less serious bargain hunters. Neighborhood and community garage sales tend to draw people who are attracted to the dynamics of the event itself. For them, the fun is in seeing who else is out shopping and looking at what everyone is offering for sale. Buying is secondary.

If you're thinking about participating in a neighborhood or communitywide event, consider the pros and cons before signing on. In general, you'll make more money during a solo sale, as you'll have less competition and distractions. However, you might also do very well at a group sale, especially if you're selling high-demand items and you're in an area with good access and visibility. Plus, you can always have a sale of your own sometime after the big event.

Insider Information

We were having a three-family garage sale in our shared driveway. The morning of the sale arrived, and neither my neighbor nor my tenant were anywhere. I was upset—I couldn't pull all this stuff and set it up alone. Finally, I threw my hands up in the air and drove to the local diner for breakfast. When I got back, everyone was bustling around setting up tables and putting stuff out, and customers were arriving. A friend came over and put my speakers in the window, and my neighbor came over with glasses and a bottle of wine. The yard sale really started cooking! By 2 P.M. my little yard was crowded with people, so we brought out more chairs for the table in the yard. People drank wine and talked, and the music played on. My neighbors came over with their children and pets. We made more than $400 that day. People started leaving at about 7 P.M., but the neighbors and friends stayed late. On Sunday, when we opened up again, the same people showed up and stayed all day again! It was the most wonderful two days I've had here, ever!

—S. from somewhere

Selling Your Own Items vs. Selling for Others

As mentioned in Chapter 3, taking items on consignment and selling them for neighbors, friends, and family is one way to increase the inventory for your garage sale. However, this is another aspect of garage sales that might be prohibited in your area. How local authorities would be able to tell consigned items from yours remains to be seen, but you might want to check the law before you agree to take in Aunt Min's old black-and-white TV or Uncle Walt's fishing tackle box.

The Least You Need to Know

- If you're new to the area or haven't yet held a sale where you live, check local ordinances and laws regulating these events.

- Pay attention to other garage and yard sales in your area to see what time of year they're held, when they start and end, the days they're held on, and how long they go for. What works for others should work for you as well.

- Consider both the benefits and drawbacks of multi-family or community sales before deciding to participate in one. Single-family sales usually generate more money for the sellers, but group events can be a good idea if your resources are tight.

Chapter 5

Organizing Charity, Rummage, and Bake Sales

In This Chapter

- Recruiting volunteers
- Finding a site
- Rounding up donations
- Getting free publicity

Of all the various ways that nonprofit groups can raise money, rummage and bake sales rank as some of the best. Not only can they be fun to organize and great to shop at, there's the special added benefit of knowing your efforts are supporting a good cause, regardless of which side of the table you're on.

Much of what goes into organizing rummage and bake sales is similar to what you'd do for your own garage sale, and you can adapt most of the information in this book to meet the needs of the particular event that you're working on. But as you'll learn in this chapter, there are some special concerns that are unique to nonprofit sales, and we've detailed them in the pages that follow.

A Really Big Show

As previously mentioned, charity sales are similar to garage sales in many ways. The things that set them apart more than anything else are their size and scope, and dealing with both factors are what make these events trickier to plan and execute well. Although small rummage sales might be about the same size as a garage sale, they always involve more people than a garage sale ever would. As sales move up in scale, they require even more people to make them successful.

Don't let these factors dissuade you from helping your favorite organization plan and execute a rummage or bake sale. The satisfaction you'll get from your efforts will be well worth the time and energy you put into them.

Putting Together the Game Plan

Just like garage sales, the key to well executed rummage and bake sales is planning. For the most part, the basic elements are the same as what goes into holding a garage sale. You'll need to pick a location, gather the inventory, promote the event, set it up, and hold it. For this you'll need a committee and lots of helpers. None of it is a one-person job.

Plan on recruiting enough committee members so you have at least one person in charge of each of the following:

- Volunteer recruitment (if you're not having each committee member recruit individually)

- Soliciting donations
- Collecting donations
- Tagging inventory
- Advertising and promotion
- Site setup and knockdown
- Staffing the sale
- Checkout

If you're having a bake sale in conjunction with your rummage sale, you'll need someone to head up that effort as well.

Try to have your committee put together a game plan at least six months before your sale. It takes a considerable amount of time to organize charity events, especially when you're dealing with volunteers who will vary in ability and commitment levels. Many organizations that have these events on a regular basis begin their planning almost immediately after the previous sale is over.

Suitable Sites

Charity sales can be held just about anywhere. Where the organization is located is an obvious choice, but by far not the only one. The following are other possible locations:

- A member's home, either outside in the garage or yard or indoors. Get more than one member of the organization to volunteer space, and you'll be able to have a larger sale and make more money.

- A park (after asking permission from the powers that be, of course).
- Other public facilities, such as schools, local government offices, churches, community recreation centers, etc.

Get creative when selecting the site for your sale. While having the event where the organization is housed can be a good promotional tool as it can introduce people to a place and a group that they may not know much about, a venue away from home base might attract more shoppers.

Trash or Treasure _____

Nail down your site as early as you can, especially if you're thinking about using a public facility. Many are booked months in advance.

Getting the Goods

Another aspect of charity rummage sales that takes a great deal of time is soliciting and gathering donations of goods to be sold. This process should also begin as early as possible so that people quit donating or throwing away items that could bring in good money at your sale.

Get the word out as soon as you can in as many different ways as possible—word of mouth, announcements at meetings, notices on bulletin boards and in bulletins, etc. It's hard to have too much to sell, but easy to have too little, and this is what will happen if you wait until the last minute to start soliciting. Tell people what you need, and tell them often.

It will be easier to get the sale set up if you sort and tag merchandise as it comes in. Try to recruit some volunteers who are willing to devote a couple hours a week or so to this effort.

Members of the sponsoring organization are usually the main contributors of inventory for the event, but they don't have to be the only source. You can also ask for contributions from other groups as well as people outside of the organization.

Ka-Ching!

Don't forget local businesses when looking for inventory for charity rummage sales. They can be great sources for quality goods that might be too shopworn to be sold as new or that are left over from past seasons.

Because you're asking people to give you things, it's always nice to give something in return. Offering to pick up donated goods is not only a nice gesture, it will increase the number of items you'll get. It can also bring in some big-ticket items that will come your way because you've made it convenient for the donors to give them up. For individuals who would rather bring in their donations themselves, arrange to have a central drop-off spot in a convenient location or set up a network of volunteers who are willing to take donations from people in their area.

Trash or Treasure

Volunteers at charity rummage sales often want to buy choice items donated by other members. Although there's really nothing wrong with this, it can keep some of the better merchandise out of the hands of the buying public, and if word gets around that your volunteers get first pick, it can diminish attendance at your sale. Set a policy on volunteer purchases—such as how many items they can buy and what they will pay—in advance of your sale, and stick to it.

Be sure to offer all donors a receipt as proof of their donation. A simple cash receipt is all that's necessary, and it doesn't even have to be pre-printed with the name of the organization—you can handwrite it or stamp it on. Just fill in the name of the donor, the date, and a brief description of the items donated, such as books, household goods, clothing, etc. Don't worry about detailing the number of items donated or their value—it's up to individual donors, not the organizations they give to, to do this. It is a good idea, however, to keep track of what was donated and by whom—both for your own records and for future solicitation purposes—which you can easily do if you use a carbonless cash receipt book.

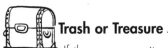

Trash or Treasure

If there are any items your organization doesn't want to sell, be sure to include this in your solicitation materials.

Telling the World

Promoting charity rummage sales and the like is similar to getting the word out on for-profit garage and yard sales. However, unlike sales held for personal gain, charity events don't have to rely on paid advertising. Placing some local ads is definitely a good idea as you want to reach as many people as possible with news of your event, but you can also get free mentions of your sale on the radio, on television, and in the newspaper. All of them are required to dedicate a certain amount of space or time to helping nonprofit organizations promote their events.

Delving into all the ins and outs of special event publicity is somewhat beyond the scope of this book. What follows is some basic information on how to contact local media outlets, which will give you a general idea of what this sort of work entails.

The first thing you need to do is get in touch with your local media—newspapers, magazines, television and radio stations—and tell them about your event. The traditional way to do this is to send written information to the media source, which usually takes the form of:

- **Calendar listings.** These short listings give the basics on your event—the who, what, when, where, and why. You can submit them to both print and electronic media.

- **Press releases.** These give more information about the event and are often used as the basis of short news stories. They also go to both print and electronic media.

- **Public service announcements.** Public service announcements, or PSAs, appear on radio and television. Station announcers may record the information, or you might be asked in to record it for them.

In each case, you'll need to find out exactly who your information should go to and the deadline for submitting your material. The quickest way to do this is to call each media outlet. Tell them who you are and who you're representing, and ask who the information should be sent to—it will vary. Ask about deadlines, which also vary depending on the medium, and if there's a preferred format that you should follow for submitting your information, especially for calendar listings and PSAs.

Make sure to follow standard formats and procedures when preparing press releases, public service announcements, and calendar listings. Also ensure that you've spelled everything correctly in your publicity materials and that all information is factual and correct.

While free publicity is great, don't rely on it as the only means for promoting your event. Your organization is one of many vying for the same space, and the amount of space you'll get isn't engraved in stone. Like you would for a personal garage sale, set a budget and identify the vehicles you think would be best for getting the word out. Because you're promoting an event that raises funds for a worthy organization, you might want to consider running display ads in addition to classifieds if your budget will allow it.

Garage Sale Don'ts

Don't send out any form of announcement until it's been read, re-read, and re-read again. You want to make sure that people don't show up a week early for your sale because you forgot to turn your calendar and gave the media the wrong dates.

Setting the Stage

Most rummage and bake sales are held in spaces that are primarily used for other purposes. Because of this, the time you get for setting up your space may be limited, which means you'll have to swing into action quickly when it's time for setting up your sale. To avoid chaos, plan ahead. Find out exactly when you'll be allowed into your space. Break down the tasks that need to be performed, such as arranging tables and racks, sorting and stacking merchandise, etc., and assign teams to each job. Tell your volunteers in advance when they should come and what they'll be doing. Put together a plan that details the physical elements of your event—where display tables and racks will be set up, where your checkout line will be located, where baked goods will be kept (if you're having a bake sale), and so on. If necessary, sketch out the physical arrangements so that everyone is perfectly clear on how the area should be set up.

You might also have to vacate your space quickly. Make sure you have enough volunteers for the back end of your sale.

Sale Staffing

You'll need a fair amount of volunteers to keep your rummage sale running as it should. Have sign-up sheets available for helpers three to four weeks in advance. Schedule people in morning, afternoon, and evening time slots so they don't get too worn out. As was the case with sale setup, assign your volunteers to specific duties, such as inventory management, customer assistance, cashiering, and so on.

Moving Merchandise Out the Door

Because rummage sales are held as fund-raisers, you want to sell as much merchandise as you can. Doing so might mean being more aggressive with your pricing—and your price slashing—than you would for a personal sale. Instead of waiting to see if you have to lower prices, develop a strategy for doing so in advance of your sale. A common plan for a two-day sale is to cut prices in half an hour or two into the second day of the sale, and in half again for the last hour or two. Another good merchandise clearing tactic is to offer a bag sale on the second day where buyers pay a set price for everything they can shove into one bag.

Also develop a plan for getting rid of merchandise left over after the sale if you can't or don't want to store it until the next sale. Possible options include the following:

- Asking donors to pick up any goods that didn't sell. It's definitely a good idea to contact anyone who donated high-ticket items.
- Letting volunteers take things for free or at greatly reduced prices.
- Donating leftovers to other charitable organizations.

Try to avoid throwing donations away unless they really aren't fit for anything other than the trash can.

If you're having a bake sale in conjunction with your rummage sale, you'll also have to plan for getting rid of leftover goods if there are any (it does happen!). Thanking volunteers for their efforts by letting them take home some goodies is a nice touch. Other possibilities include donating them to a homeless shelter or other temporary housing facility.

The Least You Need to Know

- Many of the same techniques for running garage or yard sales also apply to charity sales.

- Take advantage of public service programming to publicize your event.

- Make it easy for people to donate their goods by arranging for items to be picked up.

Chapter 6

Getting the Word Out

In This Chapter

- Proven promotional strategies
- Best advertising venues
- Wording that works
- Other ways to promote your sale

Advertising is a major key, if not the major key, to a big money garage sale. It's difficult to emphasize strongly enough the unlimited power and potential of getting the word out. The more people who come to your sale, the more you will sell. It's that simple!

All the hard work you put into a garage sale can be for naught if no one knows about your sale.

Here's a simple equation: The more people who hear about your sale, the more sales you'll make. It's that simple!

Developing Winning Ads

Lots of cars parked along your street the day of your garage sale tells other garage-salers that there's a great sale being held at your place that they absolutely, positively can't pass up. Having an effective advertising strategy is one of the best ways to drive them to your door.

Even if you do everything else right for your garage sale, if you don't devise a winning ad, you'll forfeit great profits.

Ka-Ching!

Your local newspaper can be a great source of ideas for eye-catching ads. Scan the garage sale ads for a month or so and see which ones grab your attention. If they stand out to you, they'll stand out to others as well.

Garage sale ads almost always run in a paper's classified section, along with all the ads for jobs, cars, merchandise, pets, and so on. Some newspapers set aside a special area of the classified section just for garage sale ads.

While you can place what's called a display ad in other parts of the paper, there's really not a strong reason for doing so. People are used to looking for garage sale ads in the classified section, and the rates for this section are decidedly better than in other parts of the paper. Display advertising, which offers

more options for adding eye-catching graphics and
headlines, definitely grabs more attention, but you'll
pay a lot more money for it.

Ka-Ching!

Plan to spend a little money to make a
little money when it comes to promoting
your garage sale. Paying $30 or there-
abouts is about standard for garage sale
ads. The more you can spend, the more
space you can buy.

The first step in placing your ad is getting the advertising rates from the paper or papers in which
you plan to run it. What you have to pay to place
your ad will be a major factor in how large you can
make it and in how many papers you choose to run
it in.

When you call the classified ad departments, ask for
their advertising deadlines. Most newspapers require
that ads be received several days before they're
scheduled to run. Although you might be able to
squeak in an ad an hour or two past the deadline,
you won't get it in if you miss it by a day or more.

If you're in an area that allows long garage sales,
you'll get a better turn out if you run two separate
ads for your sale. Not at the same time, but right
after each other. The psychology behind this is simple: Most people won't want to come to a sale when
they know it's already been going on for a while. If
they see an ad that's been running for five days and

it's the fifth day of the sale, they'll think that most of your stuff is already gone and that it won't be worth the drive to your sale.

 Garage Sale Don'ts

> Don't place your ad too far in advance of your sale. A day or two before the sale is good timing for ads in daily newspapers. If you're advertising in a weekly paper, the ad should run in the issue published just before your sale starts.

Instead, split the sale into two separate entities for your ads. Run one ad for three days, and another ad for the remainder of the sale; i.e., for a six-day sale, run one ad from Monday through Wednesday, the other ad from Thursday through Saturday. You'll have to place two separate ads for this, and you might have to make two separate calls to your newspaper if they won't take both ads at the same time, so don't forget to make that second call.

Breaking up the ad for a long sale into two separate ads is a proven approach that works. People will come out in droves. This method will cost you a little more for the ads, but it pays off big, especially if you have lots to sell.

Other Print Advertising Venues

Don't limit your advertising buy just to your daily or weekly paper if you can afford to run ads in

more than one publication. While it's a good idea
to concentrate your resources on the publication
that carries the largest number of garage sale ads,
the following are also possible advertising venues,
and their rates can be extremely reasonable:

- Free-distribution area shoppers.
- Senior newspapers.
- Local specialty publications that cover
  antiques shows and sellers, arts and crafts
  events, and the like.
- Monthly newsletters published by special-
  interest organizations such as craft clubs,
  quilting clubs, model-making clubs, etc.
- Church newsletters.

Insider Information

When you're calling around to get ad
rates, ask the papers if they are associated with any other newspapers in the
area, and if so, what you would be
charged if you ran your ad in those publications as well. I did this and found that I
would be charged nothing extra to have
my ad placed in every newspaper a company I called owned. It turned out that
they owned 50+ small-town papers. It
only cost $6 to place the ad in all of
these papers. Thus, it never hurts to ask.
—VBM

Publications like these are a great way to get the word out to people who might not subscribe to your local paper or who might have a particular interest in the items you're offering for sale. Advertising in senior publications or church newsletters is also a nice way to support a nonprofit organization.

Advertising on the Internet

The Internet is another medium to keep in mind when putting together your garage sale promotional plan. There are a number of websites that specialize in running garage sale ads and others that run them along with other bargain hunting information. You'll find a list of sites to consider in Appendix B.

Elements of Winning Ads

Garage sale ads are similar to other classified ads in that they usually don't have strong visual elements to attract readers to them. Instead, they're lists of the items being offered for sale. Those long lists create a lot of boring gray space in your ad unless you do something to break it up. Although your options for doing so are somewhat limited because of the classified format, there are some things you can do to bring more interest to your ad:

- **Make it longer than the others.** Yes, the extra length will cost more. However, longer ads stand out when they're surrounded by shorter ones. An ad that contains a large amount of detail will also help convince people that it's worth their while to attend the sale.

- **Use all capital letters and bold print for key words or phrases** in your ad to make them stand out. This goes against all the conventions when it comes to how ads should be composed, as type that's set in all capital letters can be more difficult to read. However, there is no denying that these techniques draw attention. So does running some key words and phrases in bold print.

- **Ramp up the punctuation.** Multiple exclamation points are also against all grammatical rules. However, it's okay to break those rules when you're putting together your ad. The idea is to do what draws attention, not what's grammatically correct.

Trash or Treasure

If you place your ad over the phone (as opposed to faxing it in), have the person taking your ad read the information back to you. Make sure all street names are spelled correctly and that all numbers—street addresses, start and end times, etc.—are correct.

If your paper offers some enhancements to its classified ads, such as special borders or small symbols, consider using these as well. Remember, you want to draw attention to your ad in every way that you can. But don't go overboard. Choose one graphic element—a border or symbols—not both.

Finding the Words

Even if you don't think you're terribly creative when it comes to writing, you'll find that creating garage sale ads is a snap. While there's no set formula to doing them, there are some basic elements to these ads that are not only essential, but that people expect to see when they read them. Start with these elements, add some detail about what you're selling, show your enthusiasm with some punchy phrasing and punctuation, and you're on your way to creating a winning garage sale ad.

Essential Information

Although it might seem obvious to include such elements as addresses, directions, etc. in garage sale ads, you'd be surprised at how many people forget to do so. Always include the following in your ads:

- Your address.
- Clear directions to your home. Make it super easy for people to get to your sale by listing major street names or intersections to help people find their way. So many people leave this information out of their ads to save money, but this is a big mistake. If there's a recognizable building or other landmark near your home, mention it, too.
- The exact days of your sale.
- The exact times of your sale.

As you'll see a bit later in this chapter, this information can be organized in several different ways.

Other Key Information

Now comes the icing. You've given the reader the basics—the who, what, when, and where. Now you want to tell them why they should come to your sale. Here's how to do it:

- Specifically name all major items you're selling. If brand names will help sell objects, list them, too.

- Specify the items that you have in quantity, such as hundreds of books, loads of toys, etc.

- Mention anything that's unique or unusual about your sale, such as vintage clothing, special-size clothing such as plus or petite sizes, collectible plates or sports cards—whatever will draw buyers' eyes and make them want to come and buy.

Always end your ad with phrases like "loads more" or "lots of misc."

Ka-Ching!

Don't waste money just ending your listing with "misc." Always add a qualifier like "lots" or "loads." This lets people know that there wasn't enough space to list everything you're going to be selling and will pique their curiosity about your other sale items.

If you're adamant about not catering to early bird shoppers, you can state this in your ad as well. Just add a line to your ad that reads "No Early Birds!" Put it at the bottom for the strongest emphasis. However, don't expect people to heed it. Some might, but seasoned garage sale shoppers are used to seeing such directives and tend to ignore them.

Samples of Effective Ads

As previously mentioned, there is more than one way to organize the information to create an effective garage sale ad. The following are all good examples of ways to do it:

1353 Valley View Road (just past Second and Vista Lane, across from Hops Drive In). OVERFLOWING! HUGE! Brand-name clothes for men, women and children size newborn to 4T. Massive amounts of toys, books, tapes, video games, computer software, baby items, bedding, gift items, microwave oven, 2 TVs, stereo, quality selection. LOADS MORE! Take Main to Second, first right past to Vista Lane. Thurs–Sat 9–3.

5975 Birdchirp Way (between Warble Rd. & Tweetie Ave). **NOT YOUR TYPICAL GARAGE SALE!** You won't want to miss this one! Over 1,000 items! Loads of toys, books, toiletries, shower massage, rugs, computer software, pots and pans, kitchen items, dishes, tools, furniture, quality clothes, infant-adult, shoes, sport cards, dishes, glassware, records, too much to mention! Mon–Wed 8:30–5.

4215 Plum Tree Circle
3 FAMILY yard sale. AWESOME!!! Pictures,
mirrors, toys, home décor, telephones, bikes,
computer software, books, games, tools, dishes,
pots & pans, clothes for all sizes, everything
imaginable! Worth the drive! Off Sweetbriar
and Sage. Take Aster to Maple to Plum Tree
Cr. Thurs–Sat 8–4.

Use punchy descriptions in your ad, but don't lie or
stretch the truth. You must have the inventory to
match your ad or you'll lose credibility and get a
bad reputation among garage sale aficionados.

Garage Sale Don'ts

What not to list in your ad? Your phone
number. Not only will you continually have
to answer the phone to answer questions
on the day of your sale, you also run the
risk of turning away potential buyers if you
don't have the specific items they're looking
for when they call to ask you about them.
Besides, why give a ton of strangers your
number when it's not really necessary?

Other Promotional Venues

Many supermarkets, hardware stores, and some
other retailers maintain community bulletin boards
where you can post flyers promoting your sale.
Make up flyers on your computer (or by hand) and
hang them on every grocery store bulletin board or

wherever they're allowed in your city. Some people visit garage sales just because of flyers they've seen stuck up somewhere.

If you're organizing a garage or rummage sale for a nonprofit organization (more on this in Chapter 5), you might be able to post flyers promoting the event in storefront windows. Some stores might even be willing to keep a supply of flyers on hand to give to interested customers.

Garage Sale Don'ts

Although it might be tempting to promote your garage sale every way you possibly can, don't go overboard and put flyers on cars or in private mailboxes. Many people find this irritating, and you might turn off potential customers.

Some communities will let you do some advance promotion on your sale by posting flyers a day or two before your sale. Check your local ordinances to see if this is permitted where you live.

Winning Signage

Signs are another key element of your promotional campaign. Be ready to make and place as many as your local regulations will allow. Remember, some people don't read the ads in the paper. All they'll have to tell them that a sale's going on are the signs that point them in your direction.

Garage Sale Don'ts _____

Many municipalities restrict the size and number of signs you can use to promote your garage sale. There might also be limitations on where you can place your signs and how long you can have them up. Check your local zoning before making and placing your signs.

You can purchase pre-made garage sale signs on wire stands or wood stakes at hardware stores and similar retail outlets. Some newspapers and real estate companies also provide these signs free to people using their services. But these signs can be pretty dull, and they often promote the place where you get them as well as your sale. Why share the space with others when you can easily make signs that will do a better job of promoting your sale?

You might have some competition for your garage sale—in fact, you probably will. So it's important to make your signs stand out from all the others that might be placed on the same spots as yours.

Sign-Making Tips

As mentioned, the best signs stand out from the others. You can make yours stand out in two ways: their physical construction and the materials you use to make them. If all the other signs are poster boards stuck to sticks, posts or poles, think about putting your signs on taller supports, which will also put them closer to the eye level of people as they drive by in their cars. You might also try the following styles:

- Putting your signs on all four sides of a large box.

- Making an A-frame sign—two tall sandwich boards attached at the top and open at the bottom. You can put your message on both sides of the sign. Be sure to include some sort of bottom brace—a long strip of duct tape connecting the bottom edges of the boards works well—so your sign doesn't start to stretch apart and collapse.

- Making your signs in different shapes. Signs in the shape of large arrows are very effective. Other possible shapes are houses, shoes (if you're selling lots of clothes), dolls (good for sales that include lots of toys), etc. Use your imagination!

Again, be sure to check your local ordinances to see what you can and can't do with your signs. There might be a very good reason why everyone's signs look the same.

If you can't (or don't want to) make your signs different from the others by how you construct them, you can make them stand out in other ways. Colorful and bright signs will always attract more attention than plain old black-and-white affairs.

Insider Information _____

Neighbors who lived about a block from us decided to have their garage sale in their garage, which was fine except that the garage faced an alley, not a main street, which wasn't the greatest for visibility. The garage, however, had been fixed up to look like a French country cottage, and if you'd ever seen it you wouldn't forget it, it was that cute. So the owners made their sale signs to look just like the garage, in the same colors and with the same details—shake roof, whitewashed walls, blue shutters on the windows, flowers in the flowerboxes, the whole bit. If you knew the garage, you knew exactly where to go. If you didn't, the signs were intriguing enough to make you want to find it.

—Sonia Weiss

This is when you want to use the most colorful fluorescent colors you can get your hands on. Go to your local craft or hobby store and buy sheets of bright green, bright orange or bright pink fluorescent poster board. Buy sturdy board, not flimsy stuff or construction paper. Choose several colors so you can use one as the background and another for making accent pieces. Use one color as the background, then cut out big arrows from another piece in a contrasting color to point people your way. Don't be afraid to combine these wild colors—a very effective color combination is a pink arrow on a green sign.

Then, use a large black marker (a dark crayon will work, too) to write something like MASSIVE SALE! or HUGE SALE! at the top of the sign. In smaller letters at the bottom, but not too small, list your address, the dates, and the times of your sale. Don't try to put too much information on your signs. Just the basics. Stick to telling people that you're having a sale, where it's going to be, and the dates and the times.

If you're selling items that appeal to a particular audience, such as computer books and software, for example, also consider making some special signs that say so. Put them up in addition to the more general signs, and don't be surprised if you draw some folks—guys, especially—who usually make sincere efforts to stay *away* from garage sales.

 Garage Sale Don'ts

> As cute as you think your kids' artistic skills might be, think twice about having them make the signs for your garage sale. Signs made by children are often illegible due to lettering that's too small or run together. You want your signs to be eye-catching and clear, not cute.

It's better to put dark lettering on bright signs than to put bright lettering on white signs. Although a brightly colored sign is definitely an attention-getter, it's hard to read bright lettering on a light surface.

You might be limited to just one sign in front of your house. If you're not, make directional signs as well as a big welcome sign to put at your house. Make them all the same color and style so people will recognize them as yours. If possible, tape them to poles high enough so people can see them from far away. Buyers in fast-moving cars need to clearly see your signs so they'll know the direction they'll need to turn in next.

Plan on having enough signs to be able to place one on every corner on every intersection leading up to your house. Starting about a mile away is a good rule for this.

Don't forget to make a large sign to put in front of your house. Many people forget this important last step. Without a sign telling people they've come to the right place, they might spend precious time looking for your sale. They also might go to someone else's. Make a yard sign that no one will miss by attaching balloons or streamers to draw attention—if they're allowed where you live.

Ka-Ching!

Take a trial drive and see if you would be able to easily find your house based on the signs you'll put up.

You might be tempted to save money and not spend very much on your signs. Get over that idea. Signs will lure impulse buyers to your sale who might or might not have seen your other ads. They'll also attract out-of-town visitors who generally don't read local papers. Good signage can make the difference between a $200 sale and a $1,000 sale. When you consider how little it costs to make them, the money you'll spend doing it is well worth your while.

The Least You Need to Know

- The more money you can spend on advertising your sale, the greater the chances of your ad reaching buyers' eyes. But don't go overboard—choose the advertising outlets that will give you the biggest bang for your buck.

- Time your ad so it appears a day or two before your sale if you're running it in a daily paper. For weeklies, the ad should run in the issue published just before your sale starts.

- Signs are a great way to grab buyers. Make yours stand out by getting creative with size, shape, construction method, and materials.

Chapter 7

Garage Sale Preparation and Setup

In This Chapter

- Pricing plans
- Sweeping clean
- Marshalling the troops
- Arranging your inventory

Have you ever heard the saying "Nothing good ever comes quickly or easily"? By now, you've probably figured out that it definitely applies to garage sales. Deciding what kind of sale to have, gathering your inventory, developing your marketing plan—it's a lot of work, it takes a lot of time, and it's enough to make you wonder if it's all worth it.

When it's time to do the final preparations for your sale, you might be wishing there were a garage sale fairy who could just swoop down and do all the work for you. Sad to say, there isn't one, but if you follow the suggestions in this chapter, your sale site and your inventory will look like you sprinkled some of your own fairy dust over them.

The week or so before your garage sale is when things swing into high gear. It's when the fact that you're doing a sale becomes a reality. Your ads appear in the local paper, your flyers go up on bulletin boards, and your signs get posted around town. It's also when you'll need to put the final touches on your inventory and get your sales site ready for all the customers who are sure to be flooding it come garage sale day.

Spiffing Up Your Inventory

Retailers get ready for big sales by counting their inventory and making sure it's in sellable condition. While inventory counting isn't necessary for a garage sale, it is important to go through everything you plan on selling to make sure it looks good, feels good, and can bring you top dollar.

It's worth spending some time and effort to ensure that all your items are clean. An old toaster oven in good working order could easily sell for $2, but it will go for more if it's shined up. Wouldn't you rather get $10 for it instead of $2?

Make sure all the clothing you're planning on selling is clean and as unwrinkled as possible.

Trash or Treasure

Even stained or torn clothes will sell if they're marked down low enough, but you'll get a better price if they're not wrinkled.

If things have been packed away for a while, unpack them so they can air out and you can assess their cleanliness and wrinkle level. Although it's not necessary for everything to be crisply pressed, definitely run an iron over anything that looks like it's been sitting in a box for the past few months.

Clothing that looks dirty or stained or smells musty should be washed. Before you throw things in the washing machine, go over them carefully. Pre-treat any stains to improve the chances of their washing out. Go through pockets for money, receipts, and other forgotten items that may be stashed in them.

Trash or Treasure

Wash garage sale clothing with scented detergent, or use liquid fabric softener or fabric softener sheets to give everything that freshly washed smell. If you don't normally use fabric softeners, or stay away from scented detergents, buy some for this purpose. Fresh-smelling clothes will sell better than things that are clean but musty smelling.

Other inventory spiffing techniques include the following:

- Running dishes and glassware through the dishwasher. Use a commercial rinse aid or add a quarter cup of vinegar to the bottom of the machine if items are grimy or filmy.

- Spraying plastic items (not ones used in the kitchen, however) and the plastic pieces on small appliances with automotive vinyl protector to make them shine and smell like new.

- Cleaning the screens on televisions, computer monitors and the like. Dust them with a fabric softener sheet and they'll stay particle-free longer.

It's always a good idea to give everything you have a final going-over before sale day. Not only does it give you a chance to make sure everything's clean, you can also check for any condition changes (cracks, chips, etc.) that could affect pricing.

If you're selling things with their original boxes, also check them to make sure they're clean inside and out. It's a great marketing technique and a nice touch to display items along with the boxes they came in, as the boxes will list all of the features for you. However, packaging that has seen better days can detract from the item it's supposed to enhance. Think twice about displaying boxes that are stained, badly torn, chewed, or mildewed.

Ka-Ching!

Always include original instructions or owner's manuals (if you have them) with such things as appliances, electronics, software, video games, etc. They can be just the thing to clinch the deal, especially on more expensive items. If you have the original boxes, include them as well.

Pricing Strategies

Should you price your goods? In a word, yes! Some people prefer not to, but why put yourself through the misery of having to come up with a price on the fly every time someone wants to buy something? Not only does pre-pricing your inventory save you a lot of time and energy on sale day, it lets people know that you're a fair seller who offers the same prices to everyone. It protects you from buyers who figure it's up to them to set the price and just plunk their money into your hand without asking you about it first. It also encourages sales from buyers who might be timid about asking prices, or who are suspicious of sellers who don't price their goods (and who might set their prices by sizing up the buyers).

Pricing is a touchy subject, and it's definitely one on which no one seems to agree. Some people will tell you to price things at about one-third of what you paid for them. Others will advise setting your price at about half of the original retail price, especially for things in good to excellent condition; and at close to 75 percent of what you paid on anything that's practically brand new. But original pricing and condition are just a part of the equation when it comes to setting the prices for garage sale goods. Seasonal goods attract better prices when they're sold either just before their appropriate season or during it. If there is a glut of items just like yours on the market, you won't be able to get top dollar no matter what kind of condition they're in.

With that said, here's our best advice:

- Remember your focus. You're having your garage sale to make money, not to just give your stuff away. Don't make the mistake that many garage sale organizers do and under-price your items.

- Look at things objectively. Even if they were expensive when you bought them, if there's not much demand for them or their condition is poor, they won't sell for much.

- Go with your gut instincts. Put yourself in the buyer's shoes, and think of what you'd be willing to pay for the item.

- Make every item you sell an individual decision. One pair of men's pants may sell for $8, another pair might only be $2. Don't set the same price for all pants or all dresses or all of one type of item.

- If you enjoy haggling, price things high enough to allow you some negotiating room.

Ka-Ching!

Don't let concerns about disgruntled buyers keep you from pricing your items appropriately. There will always be an outspoken few who will say you are charging too much, but most people are willing to pay good prices at a quality sale.

If you follow the other principles in this book, you'll be able to charge more for your items than other sellers can. For example, a lot of sellers price their paperback books for 10 to 25 cents. If you set up your sale right by following the suggestions in this book, you can sell your paperbacks for more—much more—40 to 50 cents.

Don't go solely by what you see at other garage sales—remember, many sellers underprice their goods. As a general rule, you can price items that are clearly used but in good condition at about one-third to one-half of what you paid for them. If they're practically brand new, charge close to 75 percent of what you paid for them.

Insider Information

My husband was selling a huge lot of videos. One guy went through the boxes and kept grumbling. "I've got friends who can get this stuff for free. Why are you charging $3 each? I can get 'em for 50 cents. My friends can get me this stuff for free. I wouldn't pay a dollar for these …" on and on. We finally told him to go shop at his friend's house. He told us we'd never sell them at those prices. We made more than $300 on the videos alone that day.

—D., Los Angeles

When it comes to clothing, however, you'll generally have to drop your prices lower on anything

other than children's clothes if you want to get rid
it. Adult-size clothing rarely sells well at garage
sales, no matter how good it is or who designed it.
If you're not that worried about liquidating these
items, price them competitively and be prepared to
have them passed over. You can put them up at your
next garage sale, or better yet, take them to a consignment shop where you'll get better prices for them.

Although it's difficult to give advice regarding specific
prices for specific items, you'll find some general
pricing suggestions in Appendix A. Use them for
guidance—don't take them for gospel. Always trust
your own instincts, and remember that people will
pay more for items offered at a quality garage sale,
which yours will definitely be if you follow the suggestions in this book. Don't shortchange yourself by
slapping bottom-basement prices on everything.
You can always slash them, if necessary, while the
sale is going on.

 Garage Sale Don'ts

> Some people like to color code their prices
> by using different colored labels to indicate
> various pricing levels. For instance, every-
> thing with a green label is 50 cents; every-
> thing with a blue label is $1. Although this
> might seem like a very snazzy and neat
> idea, it isn't. Most people find color-coded
> garage sales irritating. Tiered pricing also
> makes it easier for dishonest shoppers to
> switch labels on you.

Labeling Strategies

You've got two basic choices when it comes to what to use to label your goods: the cheap way or the classy way. Masking tape is the cheap way, and it looks just like it is: cheap. It takes a long time to pull and cut each piece off the roll, it won't stick to everything, and it can leave marks behind when it's pulled off. Definitely not the image you want, right?

Making individual labels from paper and sticking them on with tape is definitely classier, but it can take forever. This is an area in which spending a little money goes a long way to preserving your sanity and making a good impression on your customers. Go to your local office supply store or general retailer and buy white self-sticking labels, either round or rectangular. Buy small ones for little items and larger ones for clothing, which will give you enough room to write other important information, such as size, brand name, condition ("Like New," "Worn Only Once," or "Never Been Used") on the label.

Use a pen with a good point on it (preferably waterproof, in case it rains) and write legibly. If shoppers can't read what it says on your label, most of the time they'll be too lazy or too shy to come up and ask about the price or size. That means missed sales, and it's exactly what you want to safeguard against.

For larger and nicer merchandise, it's a good idea to think like a retailer and give these items some special promotion. Either hand-write or use your computer to make signs to identify and call attention to these items. Tell shoppers why they should stop and take a look. For instance:

Twin-Size Sheets
Brand New!
Only 9.95

Or:

Fischer-Price Tape Recorder
Only 7.95

Get the idea? Create a store atmosphere. Touches like these will make your customers willing to pay more—lots more, believe it or not.

Always put your labels where people can easily see them. If you're pricing pots, put the labels on the handles or inside them, not on their bottoms. The same thing goes for lids, glasses, plates—you name it. It also goes for clothing. Many sellers don't label their clothing well, which could be why they don't sell much of it. If you want your clothes to sell, make sure you mark each item clearly. State the exact size and price. For example, if it's a man's shirt, and it's a size 16 neck and 34 sleeve, your label should say:

Size 16 to 34
3.95 (or whatever price you've decided on)

There is nothing worse than going to a garage sale, seeing a stack or rack of clothes, and having to search inside each item to check the size. Most people won't even bother—it's too much trouble. Make it easy for people to see prices and sizes, and you'll not only sell more, you won't have people constantly asking you how much things cost.

Garage Sale Don'ts

Never mark prices directly on anything you're selling. Even washable markers can leave marks behind. And don't ever try to conceal a flaw or chip with a price tag. It's better to state "as is" on the tag than deal with an irate buyer later.

Pricing Psych-Outs

Most people know that pricing items under a whole dollar, such as $1.99 instead of $2, makes things seem cheaper. Use this trick when pricing your goods. For example, instead of $2, mark the item for $1.95. Doesn't it seem cheaper? Another psychological tip is to leave the dollar sign off your items. Just mark them as 1.95, 2.95, and so on. When people don't see the dollar sign, their minds don't immediately say "dollar." They just see the numerals and think "one ninety-five" instead of "a dollar and ninety-five cents." This is a subtle little ploy, but it does work. You will sell more this way.

Bountiful Bundles

Bundling multiple items is another proven selling technique. A solitary roll of wrapping paper might go unnoticed no matter how cheaply you've priced it, but bundle it with a bunch of other half-used rolls and they'll all find a new home. Selling like items together almost always moves them faster than trying to sell them individually. You can use this technique with just about anything—shelf paper, spools of ribbon, crayons, markers, placemats, yarn, knitting needles—you name it.

 Insider Information _____

Here's a tip for selling something that's fairly high dollar and is a popular item that appears in catalogs or sale ads. Cut out the ad with the item in it (with the price showing, of course), and tape it to your item. I've seen this done mostly with gently used children's toys and such. It shows the buyer that spending $10 for an item that normally sells for $40 new is a good idea. Be selective if you use this tactic; people will get turned off if you do it for every item you're trying to sell.

—Chris Heiska, The Yard Sale Queen

The same strategy also works with larger items that you might not have bought together but that can work as a group. Mismatched wicker furniture? Price each piece individually and you might sell them; offer them as a group and chances are better that some happy shopper will immediately take them off your hands.

Small toys are great bundling items. Fill plastic food storage bags with miscellaneous little things that your kids don't want anymore. Put a different price on each bag—45 cents, 75 cents, 95 cents, etc.— according to what you think they're worth. Children absolutely love buying up these bags of treasures.

Parents love it, too, because for a fairly low price their kids get to go home with something from a garage sale without spending too much money.

Other good bundling items include the following:

- Costume jewelry. And don't leave out broken pieces—people who collect this stuff often use the stones and findings from damaged items to repair pieces in their own collections.
- Sewing items, such as buttons and thread.
- Craft items of all kinds.
- Hardware items such as nuts and bolts, nails, and so on.

Bundling is also a good way to present silverware and cutlery that you're selling. Not only is it easier to keep track of items when they're bundled, you can protect your buyers' hands from cuts by turning knife edges toward the center of the bundle.

Staffing Your Sale

It's always a good idea to have someone help you when you're having a garage sale, and the week be-fore your sale is prime recruiting time for getting them.

A good rule of thumb is to have at least one assistant; two if it's a big sale and you have lots of merchandise out. The best helpers are often family members, but be flexible about having family around. If your husband or your kids are going to pitch a fit every time a shopper picks up an item that they are now regretting they have consigned to your sale, think seriously about packing them off for the day. Get a neighbor or a good friend to help you with the sale instead.

 Garage Sale Don'ts

> If you have very small children, don't try to baby-sit them while you're running your sale. Get someone else to watch them for the days of your sale. It can get rather hectic during those busy times.

Preparing Your Sales Site

How many times have you walked into a department store with dusty shelves and filthy floors that looked like someone had taken the oldest, ugliest merchandise they had and thrown it all over the place? Let's hope the answer is never! But, let's suspend reality for a moment and consider what it would be like to shop in a place like this. You probably wouldn't be strongly motivated to spend your money there, no matter how good the prices were. Chances are pretty good that no one else would want to, either.

Sad to say, this is exactly what some garage sales look like. But yours isn't going to! Although it's possible to make a little money at sales like these, a little money is all you'll make if you take this approach.

A clean and fresh-smelling environment is critical to successful sales. The goal is the make the garage, yard, or whatever space you're using look attractive and clean so that people will stop and shop!

Because garage and yard sales come in every imaginable shape and size, it would be impossible to give you specific setup plans. So use the information in the following sections as a guide, and don't be afraid to improvise. Nothing's engraved in stone. Do what works for you.

Getting the Garage in Gear

Most home sales are held in and around garages, so we'll begin with this area. Start by taking everything out of your garage. This will take a lot of work the first time you do it, so enlist the help of your family or friends. Remember, though, after your first sale, cleaning the garage gets easier.

Hose down the garage floor, wipe off the shelving and tables you're going to be using, and sweep out any remaining dirt or leaves. Check the garage floor and driveway for slippery spots or other hidden hazards.

Trash or Treasure _____

Have oil spots on the floor of your garage? Sprinkle kitty litter over them to soak them up, then sweep up the soaked litter.

If your garage smells musty or off in any way, now's the time to tackle odors and get rid of them. An air freshener is a good fix, although often only a temporary one. Dried eucalyptus branches usually smell better than air fresheners, and will do an equally effective job masking odors.

After you're all done cleaning, move any items you're not selling back in. Place them to one side, away from customer traffic, and drape them with sheets, blankets, tarps—whatever you have on hand that will hide them from view. People will want to buy everything they see … it never fails. If you have any valuable items in your garage, such as expensive hand tools, for example, avoid any hassles over them and put them somewhere else for the duration of your sale.

Now you're ready to do your setup. The following arrangement works well in a two-car garage; adapt it to suit the size of the space you're using:

- Arrange three rows of tables vertically, front to back. You may use large makeshift boxes of the same height and cover them with a nice blanket or sheet. Get creative; use two boxes, chairs or sawhorses with plywood spread across them as a table. Anything that will hold items will do as long as they're covered with an attractive sheet or blanket. Be sure to leave room around every table and between tables and shelves so people can move around freely.

- Place bookshelves, steel shelving, and clothes racks along the perimeter of the garage. If you don't have clothes racks, string some rope across the ceiling and use it for displaying clothing. If you have a couple of ladders, or can borrow one if you only have one, make them into a clothes rack by putting a broomstick or mop handle between them. Put two at different levels and you'll have even more room to hang clothes.

- Put a small table (card table–size) or a large box near the entrance of your garage. This is where you'll transact the sales. Drape it with a blanket or sheet so you can hide valuable items underneath it. Equip it with a pad of paper (to mark down what you sell and total it at the end of the day), a calculator, empty sacks/bags, pencils and pens to write with, a cassette or CD player, and whatever else you'd like to have to get you through the sale.

Trash or Treasure

Racks can be inexpensive and a good investment. You can get them at Target, Wal-Mart, K-Mart, and other stores at very reasonable sales prices throughout the year. As your family gets bored with or outgrows certain clothes during the year, put them on your racks for your next garage sale. That way they stay unwrinkled and are still nice looking when it's time to get them ready for your sale.

Some people like to place their cashier table at the end of their driveway, and you can certainly move it down there on sale day, but for now just get it set up and leave it inside the garage. Regardless of where you end up placing it, don't plan on spending all your time sitting at it. You'll have a much more successful sale if you and your helpers are on your feet, greeting and talking to customers. Take shifts at the checkout table when your feet need a break.

On the day of the sale, if it's nice out, you're going to drag a lot of items outside on the driveway to attract attention. However, be sure that everything you set up will fit into your garage in case of rain.

Setting Up Yard Sales

Yard sales are a little trickier to set up as you usually can't leave your tables and merchandise out overnight. It's best to do the basic preparation work in the garage (and behind closed doors, if possible, to avoid prying eyes) and move everything into place the day of your sale.

If your yard isn't flat, you'll need to find the flattest part of it for placing tables and other display pieces. Next, put away anything that could cause someone to trip, such as hoses, toys, dog stakeouts, etc. (No matter how friendly your dog is, by the way, it should also be out of sight come sale day.) Also stash anything that's breakable or that you don't want to sell, including lawn ornaments, pots, decorative stones, and what have you. Cut the grass and fill in any potholes in your turf. Inspect the yard for any doggie droppings that might have escaped your regular policing. Even if you don't have a pet, it's a good idea to check your lawn to see if other animals have left any surprises.

Setting Up Indoor Sales

Indoor sales should be located as close to an entrance as possible so people don't go traipsing through your house uninvited. If such a location isn't possible, make sure visitors know exactly where the sale is by putting up signs both inside and out that make it perfectly clear. If you want people to use your back door, for example, point them to it at your front door. Another good idea, especially if you don't want people to come in without ringing the doorbell or knocking on your door, is to put a sign that says "Please Come In" on the door you want them to use.

If the weather is bad, put up a sign asking people to take off their shoes.

Setting Out Your Wares

Having your inventory neatly arranged and well organized is the last step in creating the retail atmosphere that equates big bucks garage sales. Make sure your items are well ordered, not helter-skelter. For instance, put toys on one table, kitchen items on another. Books should go on shelves for easy browsing, but placing them spine up in shallow boxes or box tops will also work.

Clothing should be sorted by type—children's, men's, and women's. All adult clothes should be hung on racks and clearly marked. Keep men's clothes on one rack; women's on another, arranged according to size. If you have especially nice children's clothes or dresses, have a separate rack for those, lined up and according to size. If not, you can stack them in low piles on tables. Better yet, because piles always fall over and get messy: Get some boxes, all the same size and not too deep, and use them for your children's clothes. Label each box for a different size—for example, newborn to 6 months, 12 months to 24 months, 2T to 4T, and so on.

Naturally, you'll group your boxes according to the sizes you have. Don't make any stack too deep in each box or you'll tire out your shoppers before they go through the whole box. Having clothing sorted in boxes will save you a lot of time—even when the clothes get messed up, they'll at least be in the correct box according to their sizes. Still, when there's a lull in people traffic on sale day, quickly go over and straighten up the boxes. Make sure no one's thrown one piece of clothing over into the wrong box.

Finally, put fragile, breakable items on the sturdiest tables.

Getting the Signs Out

The day before your sale is a good time for posting promotional signs unless the municipality where you live won't let you put them up until sale day, or there's the possibility of bad weather. If this is the case, try to get them out at least 30 minutes before you're ready to start your sale.

Wait until the day of your sale to place any yard signs. And don't forget to make one of the most important signs you can have—the one that says "All Sales Final."

The Least You Need to Know

- Make your sale area as shopper-friendly as you can. If you're using your garage, clean it thoroughly and get rid of any nasty smells it might have. If you're using your yard, make sure it's devoid of anything that could cause someone to trip or fall.

- Pricing garage sale items can be tricky. As a general rule, you can price items that are used but in good condition at about one third to one half of what you paid for them.

- Make it easy for shoppers to buy by pricing your items clearly and by putting your stickers where they can be easily seen.

Chapter 8

Sale Day

In This Chapter

- Dealing with early birds
- Managing your cash
- Handling customers
- End-of-sale tactics

The big day is here! All your planning and hard work has come down to this moment in time. You'll soon find out whether it's all been worth it. If you've followed the advice in this book, it will be.

Before you reap the fruits of your efforts, however, you've got at least one full day's worth of work ahead of you (more if you're holding a multi-day sale). Get ready to wear lots of hats—salesperson, cashier, stocker, and security guard among them— as garage sales are definitely multi-tasking events. So take a deep breath, think ahead to how great you're going to feel when it's all over, and get ready to have a big money garage sale.

Completing the Final Setup

In a perfect world, you'll have everything in order and ready to go in your garage the night before your sale. Your display tables and racks will be in place and assembled, your merchandise will be priced, organized and stacked neatly, your checkout table will be preset with such items as a calculator, a radio or cassette player, a pitcher of water, etc., and ready to be moved into place. But we don't live in a perfect world, and it's the rare seller who is this organized.

If you weren't able to finish your preparations the day before your sale—if it's your first sale, chances are pretty good that you won't as first-time sales almost always take longer than you think they will to organize—plan on getting up early on sale day— really early, like at the crack of dawn—so you can get last-minute tasks done before your sale is scheduled to start.

A good rule of thumb is to be ready to open your sale at least 20 minutes before your stated opening time. However, even experienced sellers are rarely completely ready when people start showing up, so don't get panicked if you're not. Keep in mind, though, that the more prepared you are, the less frantic you'll be the morning of the sale. If you're having a yard sale, now's the time to move your tables and clothes racks into place. If possible, move them with your merchandise already sorted and stacked to save extra steps and time. If you're using a rope or cord to display clothing, string it up and make sure it's secure before loading it up.

Garage Sale Don'ts

> If you're using clothes racks, don't set them up where the wind can knock them down and make a mess. If you're having a garage sale, keep them inside your garage. If you're having a yard sale, put the racks close your house where they'll have some protection from the wind.

Veteran garage sale sellers have various schools of thought on where the checkout table should be located. Being close to the action at hand so you can keep an eye on everything is a given, but there is really no one best spot. Just outside the garage is a favorite place for garage sales; closer to the street is another option for outside sales of any type. Setting up where people passing by can see and talk to you is also a great way to increase shoppers at your sale. Some people will just cruise past if they don't immediately see something they want, but they'll stop if the answer is yes when they ask you if you have it.

Placing some of your hot-ticket items where people can see them as they drive or walk by is another great way to attract more customers. The end of your driveway is a good place, but they can go just about anywhere as long as the spot is visible to you as well.

Another marketing strategy is to put some low-priced items for sale outside your garage, near the street and along the driveway. Having very large and interesting items on the driveway and the front yard will entice people to actually get out of their cars and bring them inside of the garage where even more treasures are to be found.

Stocking Your Change Drawer

This is also the time to get your cash ready for making change. A good rule of thumb is to have $50 on hand, broken down as follows:

- One $10 bill
- One $5 bill
- Twenty $1 bills
- $10 in quarters
- $3 in dimes
- $2 in nickels

You won't need pennies if your prices end in zeros and fives.

 Garage Sale Don'ts

If you're using a moneybox, don't put it on your checkout table until the last second before your sale starts. Once you bring it out, never leave it unattended. Don't give anyone the chance to make off with your hard-earned cash.

Powering Up

If you're selling electrical items, put out a power strip or extension cord so people can plug them in to make sure they work. If the cords are long, tape them into position with electrical or duct tape so people won't trip over them.

Also have a supply of batteries on hand so items that require them can be tested. Don't put the batteries in the items you're selling, as you'll end up selling them with the items. Post a small sign to tell buyers that batteries for testing are available, and keep the batteries on your checkout table.

Placing Your Signs

If you weren't able to put out your sale signs the night before, get them out as early as you can the day of your sale. If the weather is blustery, have someone check them periodically to make sure they stay in place. If your sale is running for more than one day, definitely check your signs every day to make sure they're still up and looking good.

 Insider Information

Ever notice how hard a woman has to work to convince a man to stop at a yard sale? To solve this, set out an old lawn mower or power tools out front in plain view of the road, and you'll get more business. It's also smart to set up a small table with nothing but "man things"—jars full of screws and nails, electronic parts, tools and parts of tools, etc. This gives the men something to immerse themselves in while the women find all the real treasures.

—Chris Heiska, The Yard Sale Queen

Dealing With Early Birds

When you're setting up, whether in the privacy of your garage or outdoors on your lawn, it's almost a sure bet that there will be some people hovering around the perimeters of your yard, either in their cars or on foot, checking the action. Yup, they're the early birds, the most avid of the avid garage sale goers, the people who can hardly contain themselves once the sun has come up on garage sale days. And they're the reason why you have to hit the ground running on garage sale days.

It wouldn't be a garage sale if a few people didn't show up early for it. In fact, if you've written a particularly enticing ad and placed your signs in good spots, you'll probably attract lots of eager shoppers who will fly out of their cars to attack what possible treasures could be theirs the second they see any movement or when your garage doors begin to go up.

Early birds have even been known to show up the afternoon or evening before a sale starts. If you find them fluttering around your location, you'll hear all sorts of reasons why they're there, including, "Gee, I thought it started today," "I won't have the car to-morrow," "We just happened to be in the neighbor-hood," and "We'll be out of town." When you tell them they're a day early and you're in the process of setting up, they might apologize and say they'll come back the next day if they've indeed made a mistake. However, chances are better that they'll stay and try to convince you to accommodate them and let them see what you're selling.

It's important to recognize early birds for what they are. At their best, they are individuals who want to beat everyone else for first dibs on your goods. At their worst, they're pushy, boorish people who don't like playing by the rules and think nothing of invading someone's privacy just so their needs can be met. Either way, they're pretty calculated about what they do, and they're hoping that you'll be inexperienced and flustered enough to fall into their trap.

Frankly, there's no way to avoid early birds. They're part and parcel of every garage sale. You can post signs that say "No Early Birds" at your sale site, and you can even include such wording in your ads and signs. They'll still show up.

So what should you do about them? Always remember that this is your sale and you are in control. If you want to open up a little early and are ready to do so, you might want to accommodate these early shoppers. But don't let them intimidate or bully you into letting them shop if you're not ready for them. You might lose a few sales, you might not. Many early birds are lookers rather than buyers, but when they do buy they often snap up your highest priced items without saying a word about it.

When it comes to early birds who show up the day or evening before a sale starts, definitely think twice about accommodating them. Very few are worth such special treatment. If they're that interested in what you're selling, they'll come back the next day. Plus, you run the risk of other early birds driving by, seeing what's going on, and rushing up to make sure they're not missing out on something big.

Insider Information _____

> Our yard sale was advertised: Yard sale
> 9 A.M. to 3 P.M. NO EARLY BIRDS. At
> 7:15 a couple was leaning over the fence.
> They stood there for 1.5 hours watching
> our every move. At 8:30 another person
> came and they seemed to know each
> other so they chatted till we were ready at
> 8:50 A.M. All three came in a big rush.
> The first couple talked loudly to each other
> about what stuff might sell for. They quickly
> found that I knew my prices and there
> were no "gems" that they could buy dirt
> cheap and resell for a fortune, so they left
> after five minutes. After all that waiting!
>
> —J., Raleigh, North Carolina

No matter what time you start letting people go
through your goods, there's really no turning back.
Your sale is in progress whether you're ready or not.

Caring for Your Customers

If you've never had a garage sale before, be prepared to meet lots of different people. Many of
them will be as nice and considerate as you could
possibly want, but they won't all be on their best
behavior. Some won't agree with your pricing and
will make their opinions known to everyone within
earshot. Some might not speak the same language
as you do and will get belligerent because you can't
understand them. Others will simply be thoughtless

or careless in other ways, such as letting their kids run rampant through your sale area or tossing around items every which way when they're going through them. Still others will want you to accommodate special needs, ranging from putting items on hold to using your bathroom (yes, it happens, and more often than you think!).

Insider Information

At our yard sale there was a middle-aged couple. While the woman looked around, the man asked if he could use our bathroom. Reluctantly, I agreed. Well, he was gone for quite a while, so I thought I would step inside to make sure he wasn't going through my stuff. All of the sudden, I hear a voice from the bathroom. "Hey, you don't have any toilet paper in here!" Embarrassed, I handed him a roll through the door. He finally finished up, and left with his wife. Neither bought anything. I walked into the bathroom later, and I won't go into details of how awful it was in there, but you get the idea. Next yard sale, no one gets past the front porch.

—M., Lawrence, Kansas

Since it's your garage sale, you're the one with the chief responsibility for making people feel welcome and providing a pleasant environment for them to shop in. Treat people the way you like to be treated.

Greet them as they come up and talk to them a little if it seems like they're in the mood for some chitchat. Keep an eye on shoppers as they go through your merchandise and offer some information on items they seem particularly interested in. Don't overdo this however—people rarely appreciate overeager salespeople who hover over them, regardless of the setting.

Other ways to make people feel welcome and enhance their shopping experience include the following:

- Serving coffee on cold mornings and making water available on hot days.

- Supplying grocery and shopping bags for buyers to carry their purchases away in. It's also a nice touch to have a roll of paper towels or a sack of newspapers on hand for cushioning fragile items.

- Providing information to people about the location of the closest public rest room. If you're having an outside sale, you should never let anyone go into your home, no matter what the reason. If nature is calling, help them out by directing them to the nearest public facilities. Follow the same approach for indoor sales by closing—and locking, if possible—the bathroom door if it's close to your sale area.

- Keeping your sales tables neat and orderly. No one likes to paw through messy stacks of clothing and other merchandise. Get into the habit of straightening your tables often.

Not only will it make them look nicer, it will give you (or your helpers) more opportunities to talk with your customers.

- Refreshing your inventory often. Unless it's toward the end of your sale and you don't have much left to sell, bare sales tables will make people wonder how committed you are to having a good sale and drawing their patronage. If you're running low on things to sell, consolidate your merchandise and remove unneeded tables.

- Leaving enough space around tables and racks for people to move freely. The average woman wears a size 14. Don't set up your tables to accommodate a size 2. Along these lines, make sure that your merchandise is accessible. If people are having a hard time reaching certain items, move them to a better spot.

- Playing some background music. Pleasant tunes in the background add a wonderful ambiance to garage sales and make people feel relaxed and welcome. It also gives them a little privacy should they want to discuss items or prices with you or their shopping companions. Choose an easy listening station or your mellowest CDs or tapes. No heavy metal or gangsta rap.

Always remember that you can't please everyone. Nor can you suit everyone's tastes and needs when it comes to what you sell. Lots of people who come to your sale might walk away without buying a thing.

What you want, however, is for them to walk away with a good feeling about their experience and about you as a seller. If they do, they'll come to your next sale.

Handling Hagglers

No matter how competitively you price your items, there will always be shoppers who will want to buy them for less. Just like early birds are part and parcel of the pre-game for garage sales, you'll have hagglers on the playing field while your sale is in progress.

Trash or Treasure _____

> Even if you don't like the haggling process, it's a good idea to be a little flexible about it, especially if your sale is winding down and you don't want to hang on to things until the next sale. Many sellers knock down their prices a bit in the waning hours of their sales. If you have a buyer who is interested in purchasing a large number of items, it can be worth your while to come down a little on your prices to facilitate the sale.

If you feel you've priced your items appropriately, and your sales are supporting this; i.e., people are buying, not walking away shaking their heads, then you may not want to haggle at all. If so, be firm about it. Put up a sign to that effect. Some people will still ask you to come down on your prices under the "if you don't ask, you don't get" theory. Just tell them no. Chances are they'll buy the items anyway if they want them badly enough.

Most sellers don't mind a little friendly bargaining, and they make some room for it in their pricing. But don't let yourself get bullied into giving up your goods for less than what you want for them. Decide before your sale what your rock bottom prices are, and stick to them.

Insider Information

> I always mark my items high enough so I have room to come down on prices. Some people enjoy negotiating!
>
> —Cathy Pedigo

Dealing With Disruptive Customers

The more effort you put into making your sale fun and enjoyable, the less you'll have to deal with people who can make it anything but. However, you can count on having at least one or two customers who you'll wish were shopping at someone else's sale. They might just be pushier than you'd like about bargaining or a little too vocal about your pricing. If you're really unlucky, however, they can be the customers from hell who are nasty enough to threaten you or your property.

One of the best ways to guard against these unsavory individuals is to make sure you don't go it alone on sale day. Have some people help you while your sale is underway. It's always a good idea to have at least two people working a garage sale—one to greet customers, keep merchandise straightened and so on, the other to staff the checkout table. If you're the diminutive type and your helper happens to be a big, burly guy, so much the better. Regardless of physical size, however, there's always strength in numbers, and it's nice to have someone on your side when you're dealing with someone who's being ornery.

Other ways to disarm disruptive shoppers include the following:

- Standing your ground. Let the person have his or her say, then quietly speak your piece. Don't argue.

- Ignoring them. If they aren't in your face, just focus on something else. They'll usually spin out on their own.

- Letting them have their way. If they're getting bent over some cheap little item, it might be easier to just let them have what they want.

Always be polite but firm when dealing with people who are causing trouble. However, if anyone becomes abusive or starts to threaten you or other shoppers, don't hesitate to ask him or her to leave. If you have a cell phone or a cordless phone, keep it at hand. If necessary, call the police.

Insider Information

In my hometown, there is an antiques dealer well known for pulling stunts at all area yard sales. When I had mine, scheduled for Saturday, the doorbell rang on Friday. There she was, saying she wanted to preview our stuff. I sternly told her that the sale was tomorrow and sent her away.

The next day, as I was setting up a tent for the yard sale, she arrived two hours before the start time. She walked past me into my garage. I told her we weren't open yet and again sent her away. When she came back hours later, she offered me $2 for a chair priced at $10. She then picked up a bowl marked $1, took the price tag off and offered me 25 cents for it. Again I refused her offer and told her I saw her take the tag off. She then asked my wife if she'd take 25 cents for it! Last, she offered me 50 cents for a bookend priced at $3. Again, I refused her petty amounts. She said that one bookend is worthless. I replied that if I had both, I'd be charging $20.

About a month later, I went to her antiques shop. I saw the bookend, marked $10. I asked her if she'd take 50 cents for it. She said it was very valuable. I replied, "That's funny. When you tried to buy it from me for 50 cents, you told me it was worthless!"

—M. G., Wallingford, Connecticut

Thwarting Theft

Fortunately, most people who frequent garage sales are honest sorts, but thefts are not unheard of. Technically, it isn't shoplifting as you're not operating a business, but for simplicity's sake we'll refer to it as such here. Most of the time you won't notice that something's missing until the end of the sale, but if you're keeping a good eye on your customers you might be able to catch the theft when it happens.

If you do spot suspicious behavior going on, call attention to the suspect—or suspects, as shoplifters often work in pairs—in some way. Go over and start dogging their every move. Ask them what they're interested in, and keep offering your help as they move around your tables. If there's indeed something fishy going on, they'll realize that you're on to them and they'll leave. If you're mistaken, you do run the risk of running off a good customer or two, but it's better to avert the problem before it starts than to try to apprehend a shoplifter.

Other shoplifting ploys to be aware of include the following:

- Customers who put the items they want to buy into a bag and tell you that they've "pre-totaled" everything when they come to pay you. They're hoping you'll either be too busy or too trusting to want to go through the bag and total the items yourself, but this is exactly what you should do.

- Price switching. This is a hard one to refute once it happens, as the suspect will almost always argue with you and tell you that you're mistaken when you say that the price is wrong. If there's more than one item, you might be able to compare the piece in question with others that do have the correct prices on them. If not, you may have to sell it at the wrong price.

- The distraction scheme. This requires shoplifters to work in pairs or groups. While one or more distract the seller, the others make off with the goods.

Garage Sale Don'ts

Think twice before accusing someone of shoplifting. There are legal and physical risks involved in doing so—legal if you're mistaken about what you saw, physical if the person decides to take you on or accuses you of having done so. If the item you suspect of being stolen isn't worth very much, it's often better to let it go and focus on getting the person off your property as soon as possible.

It's always a good idea to balance your actions with the amount of risk involved when dealing with shoplifters. If a small item was taken, it's often not worth drawing attention to the problem and upsetting other customers. If you do confront a suspected shoplifter, tell the person what you saw and ask for the merchandise to be returned. If the individual resists, tell him or her that you're calling the police and ask the suspect to stay until they arrive.

If the suspect flees, try to get the license number. Keep in mind, though, that the theft has to be fairly substantial for the police to want to get involved. Even if they do, it will be difficult to prove ownership once the shoplifter has left your property unless the stolen goods have identifying marks or serial numbers that you can verify.

The good news about shoplifting is that it doesn't happen very often and the items taken are usually insignificant. The best way to guard against anything of value being taken is to not sell it in the first place or place the item where you, or someone helping you, can watch it throughout the sale.

Managing Your Cash

As your sales day gets underway, cash will start flowing in. To keep the amount of money you have to work with at a manageable level, don't keep much on hand beyond the $50 you started with. As your cash box or apron or fanny pack fills up, take your profit out and stash it somewhere safe, preferably in your house where there's no chance of someone else finding it. An even better idea is to run it to the bank.

If you're taking in a lot of large bills (almost guaranteed to happen if you have a sale right after pay day), you might want to hang on to a couple $20s and a few more $10s than what you started with.

Most garage sale shoppers know the rules of the land and won't even attempt to pay you with a check. However, some people might want to pay with a check if they're buying expensive items.

Trash or Treasure

If you're handed a large bill, leave it on your sales table while you're making change and keep it there until you've handed the change back to the buyer. If you don't, the buyer could lie and say that he or she gave you a larger bill. Sad to say, there are people who will do this. Don't give them the opportunity to try this little ploy.

The best advice on accepting checks is not to unless you know and trust the person on the other end of the pen. It's just too hard to collect the money from people who write bad checks, and you might even find that you've been given a check that was drawn on a closed account. Most people are trustworthy. Some definitely aren't. Sadly, there are some people who can be that dishonest.

If you're adamant about a cash only sale, state it in your ad and post a sign to that effect the day of your sale. If you do decide to take a check, ask for identification and a credit card. Write both numbers on the check. If a phone number isn't printed on the check, ask for it as well.

Keeping Things Safe

Security generally isn't much of an issue at garage sales, but it's always best to be on your toes any time you have strangers coming to your home. If you're having your sale on your own (never a good idea,

by the way, but sometimes it can't be helped) put
on some loud music or leave a television on inside
to give the impression that someone else is home.

Because you have to be greeter, stocker, and
cashier, consider dispensing with the money box
and coming up with a way to stash your proceeds
on your body instead. Some sellers just keep their
money in their pockets, but this isn't a good solu-
tion if you have a lot of change. A better alternative
is a fanny pack, a carpenter's apron, or just a regular kitchen apron with pockets if it's made out of
fairly sturdy material. A side benefit to wearing an
apron: It will also keep your clothing cleaner.

Other ways to protect you, your merchandise, and
your home from harm include the following:

- Never allowing anyone in your house, or, if
  you're having a sale inside your house, never
  allowing anyone to roam outside of your
  sale area.

- Keeping things of value where you can
  watch them.

- Not displaying merchandise such as videos,
  CDs, or computer games that are tempting
  for sticky fingers. Instead, put out the empty
  boxes with notes telling customers to ask
  you for the items. You can keep the games
  in the house if you have a helper, or in a box
  behind your checkout table.

Never leave your garage sale unattended. If you're
on your own during your sale, don't help people
carry things to their cars, and don't for any reason

go into your house. Protect your home by locking the doors, and make sure anything of value in your garage is either stowed away or covered up. Don't give people opportunities to take advantage of you.

Calling It a Day

If your sale is like just about any other garage sale ever held, you'll get your best customer counts in the earliest hours and you're going to be your busiest assisting all those buyers who are snapping up your goods. As the hours trickle by, sales will slow down, and you might be so dog tired that you want to mark everything down to next to nothing so you can get rid of it and end your sale early. Good idea? Probably not.

 **Insider Information**

> I don't worry about not selling certain higher-priced items the first time around. Usually, by the second or third time I put them up for sale, somebody will come along who will pay full price, or close to it, for my prized items.
>
> —Cathy Pedigo

If you're willing to hang on to your merchandise until you have another sale, you'll probably sell it for what it's worth. And as tired as you are, it's best to keep your sale going for the entire advertised time if you have enough merchandise on hand to do so. Some of your biggest sales might come in the hour or two before you planned to close up shop. On the other hand, you may end up twiddling your thumbs. Of course, if you're completely out of things to sell, or just about out, definitely shut down early. You've earned it, and it's not worth staying open just to sell a few more things.

If people are still coming up after your stated closing time, it's up to you to decide whether you want to stay open for them. If you're tired, tell these last minute shoppers that you're closing down for the day but that you'll be open the next morning (if you're scheduled to be). There's no rule that says you have to stay open if you don't want to. However, there might be one that says you have to shut down at a certain time. If there is, tell folks you're complying with the law and your sale is over.

The Least You Need to Know

- If you haven't finished setting up for your sale the night before, plan on getting up early on sale day to tackle whatever's left to do.

- Open your sale when you're ready. Don't let early birds badger you into starting early unless you really want to.

- Never let anyone roam through your home unsupervised. Know the location of the nearest public restroom, and be prepared to give directions to it should anyone need to know.

- Don't keep more cash on hand than what you need to work with. As money flows in, stash it away, either in a secure place in your home, or, better yet, at the bank.

Chapter 9

Successful Buying Strategies

In This Chapter

- Turning your thinking around
- Mapping your route
- Sale-day strategies
- Knowing when to keep your mouth shut

If you're a garage sale aficionado—if you're reading this book, chances are pretty good that you are— the following scenario or one similar to it is bound to happen to you (or already has):

> You're tootling along on a bright Saturday morning without a care in the world, going about your normal weekend routine, when you suddenly see a great looking garage sale sign. Within seconds, you've whipped your car around in search of the sale that belongs to that sign. Within minutes, you're happily digging into piles of things that look almost embarrassingly similar to what you sold at your last garage sale.

Red-faced? Don't be. If you enjoy having garage sales, it makes sense to enjoy shopping at them as well. In fact, being a garage sale shopper serves a dual purpose if you also hold them on a regular basis. Not only might you find some great bargains that you'd otherwise miss out on, you also might pick up some great ideas for making your next sale better.

Putting On Your Buying Cap

If you know the basics behind putting on a successful garage sale, you're almost assured of being a whiz at shopping at them. For the most part, it just takes a different mind set—flipping around what you already know about them so you're looking at things as a buyer instead of as a seller. As a seller, you set up early. As a buyer, you arrive early. As a seller, you make sure you have enough small bills and change. As a buyer, you carry small bills so you don't have to inconvenience a seller by asking for change for a $100 bill when you're buying a 25-cent item (which, by the way, is a nasty little buying technique that won't win you any friends but might have you walking away with the item for free because the seller would rather get rid of you than change such a large bill).

Although most of the selling techniques you learn when holding garage sales will put you in good stead as a buyer at them, there are some techniques that are unique to buying.

Planning Your Attack

As a seller, you went to great lengths to create a winning ad to attract buyers. As a buyer, you're going to use those ads to determine the sales that are worth going to.

The best garage sale shoppers map out a systematic plan of attack that yields them the best results in the shortest amount of time. Here's how to do it:

- Scour local newspapers and other media for sale ads. Circle the ads that look most intriguing as well as ads for sales that you might want to hit if you have the time.

- Use a street map of the area to determine where the sales are going to be held. (If you don't have a detailed street map, you can get maps and directions to specific locations on the Internet. Do a search for "maps," and you'll find several sites that offer this information.) Mark each sale location with a pen. You might want to use different colored pens to indicate the sales you definitely want to hit and sales that you think might be worth checking out if you have the time.

- Connect the dots. Starting at your house, figure out the best route to the sales that interest you the most, then for the sales that you're not as interested in but will stop at if you have the time and inclination (and if you haven't already spent all your money).

Once you've figured out your route, it's helpful to sort the sales into one list, starting with the first sale you plan to go to. One way to do this is to cut out the ads and paste them all onto one sheet of paper (use more than one, of course, if you can't fit them all onto one). If you don't have time to mess around with little cut-outs or plain don't want to, number the ads in the order in which you plan to go to them, fold the page they're on into a manageable size and clip it to a clipboard.

Insider Information

> To avoid having to cut out all the little ads in the newspaper, or wasting time copying them to a sheet of paper, here's a better idea: Take a piece of transparent tape and place it over the ad. Using your fingernail, rub the tape over the ad several times. Then carefully lift the tape and place it on a sheet of paper. All the information will be transferred to the tape. You may want to do a practice one first. (This technique won't work with all newspapers, by the way, as some inks don't transfer.)
>
> —Chris Heiska, The Yard Sale Queen

Matching Your Needs to the Sales

Just like your garage sales can't be all things to all people, there are going to be sales that are better than others at yielding the items you're after.

Knowing what you want, and matching the sales to your needs, is a great way to determine which sales you want to go to. For example ...

- Garage sales held in fancy neighborhoods will generally have better goods than those that are not. But here's a secret about these sales: You can get some great bargains at them. Although it's always folly to make sweeping generalities about such things, especially when times are rough, people with higher incomes are often more concerned about clearing away clutter and getting rid of unwanted items than they are about making lots of money doing so.

- The same philosophy holds true for rummage sales held by churches and other nonprofit organizations, but for a slightly different reason. Members of the church or organization usually donate the items at these sales. Because the profits from the sale are generally used to fund various charitable efforts, building improvements and the like, the members are encouraged to donate items in good condition and with decent values.

- If you don't have kids at home, it doesn't make much sense to go to sales in areas populated by young families as these sales will primarily focus on clothing and toys for little ones. You might find other worthwhile items at them, but not in numbers great enough to warrant spending large amounts of time at them. The reverse is true if you're looking for kids' things. Skip sales in neighborhoods where you don't see swing sets and trikes dotting the landscape.

- If you're looking for housewares, used furniture, and other household items such as appliances and fixtures, focus on sales held in neighborhoods populated by older residents, say in the 40- to 60-year-old range. These individuals often sell perfectly good items that they've tired of or want to upgrade and have either replaced them or are getting ready to do so.

Keep in mind, however, that there's always going to be those garage sales that are the exceptions that prove the rule. Don't be too quick to draw conclusions about what you'll find at garage sales held in various areas of your community. If the description of a sale looks good, go for it regardless of where it's being held. That young family with three kids and a fourth on the way might be selling Gram's Roseville vases that they inherited, have no room for, and can't stand the sight of. You might find great baby clothes at a sale held by an older couple whose daughter and young family moved before they had the chance to sell their items themselves.

Also, don't be too quick to judge a sale that's not organized as well as yours are. Most people don't know how to plan and hold a successful garage sale, or take the time to do it, and their sales are going to reflect this. You might be tempted to leave when you see clothing strewn willy-nilly on the ground or appliances and household goods that reflect the owner's unfamiliarity with the term "elbow grease," but this doesn't mean that the merchandise isn't worth looking at.

Insider Information

My husband and I went to a yard sale where the stuff for sale was left behind by a tenant who had left no forwarding address. There was a box of dirty white dishes that had a raised pattern on them. Not knowing if they were of any value, but thinking they were pretty, I asked "How much?" She said $5 (I was going to offer her $10). I paid her and took the box home and cleaned them up. Noticing the stamp "Wedgwood" on the back, I called my mom to see if she knew anything about it. When I told her what I had, she said "Whaaat! Wedgwood!!! That's the blue and white collector stuff." I decided to look into what I had and found that I had stumbled upon $1,000 of china! This only fed my addiction to bargain hunting.

—K. in Washington

Sale-Day Strategies

A lot of what you're going to do on sale day is common sense. It's a given that you're going to get there early so you can snap up the best merchandise before anyone else gets there. You're going to wear comfortable shoes and clothing layers that you can peel off as the day gets warmer (you are, aren't you?). So we'll dispense with the obvious advice here and instead clue you in on some insider tips gleaned from the pros that will make you a pro at shopping at them as well:

- Athletic shoes made out of leather and mesh are just about the best thing out there for shopping at garage sales. Many buyers prefer them to canvas sneakers as the canvas gets squishy wet when you walk across dewy lawns in the early morning. The thick soles of athletic shoes will keep your feet drier. They also beat sandals hands down. Wouldn't you rather have hot feet than blistered feet?

Trash or Treasure _____

If you're shopping for clothing for yourself, wear close-fitting clothing that you can easily slip things over, such as a T-shirt and nylon athletic pants, so you can check sizes without having to duck into a dark corner. If it's a cool day, wear a long sweatshirt as a top layer. If it's hot and you're uncomfortable shopping while so scantily clad, wear a loose long shirt.

- Don't carry a purse. Keep your money in your pants pocket, or, better yet, in a fanny or belt pack. Dorky, yes, but it's better than having to worry about an accessory that can get stolen—and it does happen. Purses on long straps can also swing into fragile items and break them. It might not happen very often, but when it does, the item that's broken is almost always something you'd never buy, but of course are now obligated to purchase. Fanny or belt packs are also good for carrying lip salve, sunscreen, sunglasses, a water bottle and anything else you might need during a long day in the sun.

- Don't plan on sellers having such things as batteries and power strips for testing electronics and appliances. Yes, they should. You would. But lots of people don't know this good seller tip. Be prepared by having your own on hand. Better still, put together a small garage sale kit that contains all the tools you'll need, such as a magnifying glass or loupe for viewing pieces close up and a black light for detecting hidden cracks in dishes and other porous objects. A pack of baby wipes or a bottle of hand sanitizer is also a good item to include. Keep the kit in your car (sans batteries, which can burst when temperatures get too high).

- Do carry a canvas tote or mesh bag to place your items in. Many sellers will look at you funny if you ask them for a bag. (If they're smart, though, they'll have them at their next sale.) Also put a tote or a box in the trunk of your car along with some soft items, such as blankets or towels, to cushion fragile objects and keep them from rolling around.

Trash or Treasure

If you're shopping at a sale where you can fill a bag full of clothing for a set price (church rummage sales are famous for these kinds of sales), don't just throw the items you want into your bag. Maximize the space by gathering up everything you want to buy first. Once you have your pile together, go through it and roll up each item as tightly as you can. Roll thin items together—such as shirts and T-shirts—to save even more space.

- Do haggle over prices. You might not like it as a seller, but guess what? It's part and parcel of garage sales, and the people you're buying from might not hate it as much as you do. If you feel an item you're interested in is priced fairly, give the seller a break and just pay up. If not, definitely offer to pay a lower amount. The worst you'll hear is "no."

- If there's something you like but you're not quite sure you want to buy it, pick it up and carry it with you until you decide. If you don't, it's almost a sure bet that someone else will scoop up the object of your desire at the exact second you decide you do want it.

- If you have lots of sales you want to go to, see if you can get a friend (or even your spouse) to preview some of them while you shop at others. If you're both carrying cell phones, you can trade information on the spot.

As previously mentioned, much of what you'll do as a buyer is predicated on what you know about garage sales from the seller's point of view. Don't toss out the rule book just because you've switched sides. Don't offer to pay with a check if you wouldn't take them yourself. If you're adamant about not putting things aside for buyers at your sales, don't ask a seller to do it for you unless you're darned sure you're going to come back to buy.

Trash or Treasure

If you're sure you want an item but don't have enough money to cover the price, give the seller what you do have and ask for a signed bill of sale. If possible, take a piece of the item with you—a handle, a drawer, a lid, a couple dishes from a set, one shoe of a pair—anything you can to insure that the seller doesn't resell the item, whether accidentally or (sad to say) on purpose. It does happen.

Special Shopping Considerations

Shopping at garage sales is so much fun that it's hard not to just dive in. And you know what? Joining the fray is perfectly okay! There are times, though, when it pays to be a little savvier and a little better prepared than your fellow shoppers.

Shopping for Kids

First, think twice about bringing very young children along with you. Garage sales, sad to say, don't rank as top little kid activities. They might be fascinated for a minute or two, but the fascination often wears off pretty quickly. Children are notorious for their short attention spans, and those spans are almost always shorter when they're doing something they don't like.

Need more reasons to leave the kids behind? Here are just a few:

- If you spend too much time keeping an eye on your little ones, you'll have less time for scoping out great bargains.

- You won't have to hide your purchases from them (or figure out a fast explanation for them) if you're buying toys for birthday or holiday presents.

- Grabby little hands and fragile objects don't go together. Remember the old saying "if you break it, it's yours"? Don't expect a seller to let you off the hook just because your kid did it. Even if she does, you should still offer to pay for the item. Think how you'd feel if it happened at your sale.

- Teenagers can be a little silly about wearing used clothing, but garage sales are great places for finding things like ski jackets, jeans, and other apparel that they'll love. If your teens aren't with you when you're buying the goods, they may not put up quite as much resistance when you unfurl your great finds.

If you're concerned about finding the right size clothing for your children if you don't bring them with you, bring their clothes instead. Tuck a T-shirt, a pair of jeans, or whatever you're trying to find in your fanny pack or tote and use them as a sizing template. If you're looking for shoes, draw an outline of a shoe that fits.

Shopping for Men

Men are also notorious for not liking to spend their time at garage sales. However, they're usually pretty frugal about their money. If your guy doesn't like to go to sales, but is amenable to buying used merchandise, ask him to give you a list of things to keep an eye out for, such as used tools, small electronics, hobby items, appliances, and the like.

Shopping at a Friend's Sale

If you're going to a friend's sale, treat it like any other sale. Don't show up before the sale starts expecting to be greeted with open arms. If the last minutes before your sales are always frantic, it's a good bet that your friend is going through the same antics preparing for hers.

If you're an old pro at holding garage sales, and your friend isn't, it might be difficult to refrain from offering some expert advice if there are aspects of her sale that need some improvement. Unless she asks for your input, however, you're better off not offering it. Tension can run a little high during garage sales, especially if they're well attended, and the most easygoing friend can get a little shrewish, especially if she doesn't have enough help. It's appropriate to offer to lend a hand if she's scrambling and you feel like sticking around. Bringing her a cup of coffee or a soft drink and something to eat is also a nice touch if she's looking tired.

Garage Sale Don'ts

Some people think it's a good idea to try to preview a friend's sale before it starts. Here's why it's not: You might end up spending more for the items you buy. If your friend senses that she's underpriced some items because you're salivating over them, chances are pretty good that she'll quote you a higher price than what she was originally planning to sell them at.

What you don't want to do is suggest ways in which she could better organize her goods, although you might be able to improve her organization a little bit by pretending to go through some of her items and surreptitiously neatening them up. You also don't want to tell her that her pricing is off if it is. If her prices are low, take advantage of them if there's something you want. If you don't, someone else will. If they're too high, just keep your mouth shut. She'll hear it often enough from other sale-goers. If her sale doesn't go well, she might ask you why after it's over. That's the appropriate time for offering some gentle advice on how she can do it better the next time.

The Least You Need to Know

- Don't prejudge a sale based solely on location. If a sale description looks good, go!
- Maximize the time you spend going to and shopping at garage sales by mapping out your route ahead of time.
- Don't offer unsolicited advice at a garage sale. It usually isn't appreciated.

After the Sale

In This Chapter

- Striking the set
- Packing it in
- Reviewing your efforts
- Planning your next sale

Whew! You did it! Your garage sale is over. If you're like virtually everyone who's ever had one, you're bone tired, and the last thing you want to think about is more work. Unfortunately, however, your work isn't done quite yet.

But here's some good news: You've already done just about everything you had to do to have a successful garage sale. Now all you have to do is get things back to the way they were before you had your sale. Oh … and count your money!

Shutting Up Shop

The very first thing to do after your sale is over is to make sure that people know you're done selling.

One of the best ways to do this is to immediately take down all your signage, both at the sale site and around town. Not only will doing this send a strong visual cue that you're done for the day, it minimizes the risk of people showing up hours or even days after the sale is over. Besides, it's simply the right thing to do.

Some municipalities require sellers to have their signs down within a certain period of time. Even if your municipality doesn't have these requirements, do everyone a favor and get them down fast.

If you put notices up on community bulletin boards, make sure they come down as well. Some places will take care of removing flyers once they've expired, but it's a good idea to go around and ensure they're removed as soon as you can.

After your signs are down, start packing up everything you didn't sell, and remove all tables and other display items from the sale site.

Be prepared for some last minute shoppers to come around as you're calling it a day. These stragglers often make the rounds of sales as they're winding down in hopes of finding things that sellers are willing to let go for next to nothing or free just to get rid of them. If you feel like letting them hang around and look at things while you're packing up, go ahead and do so. You might get an extra sale or two, which is always a good thing. On the other hand, if you've had enough of the garage sale experience and you don't want to drag out your sale any further, just tell them that you're done for the day and you're keeping everything that's left for your next sale.

Packing Up

Hopefully you've had an extremely successful sale and you don't have much remaining on your display tables. If you are left with inventory on your hands, however, you'll have to spend some time putting it in boxes or putting things back in your home. Again, this is the last thing you'll want to do if you're exhausted. However, if you're planning on having another sale it's worth the extra time and trouble to pack things up instead of just throwing them into boxes under the premise that you'll sort everything out later. Later usually doesn't come until you're getting ready for the next sale, and it will be a lot easier to prepare for it if things are packed right the first time.

The easiest way to pack up is to keep items together in the same categories you put them in when you were arranging your sale tables. If necessary, cushion fragile items in boxes. If you have plastic bags left over from your sale, use them for padding and you won't have to worry about gathering them up again for your next sale.

Clothing on hangers should be stored on clothes racks or in closets. If you used boxes to display children's clothes, all you'll have to do is refold any items that need it and seal the boxes up. If it's going to be awhile before your next sale, put something in the boxes to keep the contents smelling fresh. A dryer sheet works well for this.

If it's humid where you live, also consider adding a desiccant pack to each box to keep things from getting musty. You can make your own with silica gel bought from a craft store (it's the same stuff that's used to dry flowers). The best desiccant has a pink/blue color indicator system that shows how much moisture is being absorbed. Put it in a small plastic bag that you've poked a couple holes into. When the color changes from blue to pink, it's time to dry out the gel. Shake it out of the bags onto a cookie sheet and place it in an oven on a low heat for a few minutes until it turns back to blue. It can be reused over and over again.

 **Trash or Treasure**

If you're using racks to store your clothes, buy a rack cover to keep items dust free, or throw an old sheet over them.

Disposing of the Leftovers

After you've uncluttered your house, you may not want to add clutter after the sale by hanging on to the things you didn't sell. Although it can definitely be to your advantage to keep your merchandise if you plan on having another sale, as it may very well sell the next time, there's nothing preventing you from getting rid of it, especially if you don't have room to store it or you simply don't want to be burdened with it.

If you're in the "everything goes" mode, remember the premise that one person's trash is another's treasure. Many charities will take unwanted items off your hands; some will even come to your home and pick up everything you want to get rid of. Donating is preferable to just throwing things out, and you'll get a receipt for tax purposes when you do.

You can deduct up to $250 worth of noncash property without having to provide written documentation to the federal government. If the fair market value (defined by Uncle Sam as "what the item would sell for at a garage sale, a flea market, or a second hand or thrift store") exceeds this amount you'll need both a receipt from the organization you gave your stuff to as well as an itemized list of the items.

If you have lots of books to get rid of, consider donating them to a library or to an organization that holds book sales as fund-raisers.

Planning Your Next Sale

Your sale is over. The dust has settled, and your profits are pocketed. Maybe you've used the money from your sale to go on a family vacation, or to buy something you've needed for a long time but couldn't afford. Pretty nice to have the extra cash, right? Made it all worthwhile, right?

So here's the big question: Knowing what you now know, both good and bad, will you do it again?

If the answer is yes, then it's not too early to start planning and preparing for your next garage sale!

Reviewing Your Sale

It's always a good idea to plan a repeat event by reviewing what you did for the last one. So take some time to critique your efforts. Do it as soon as possible after your sale is over, and write down everything—the good and the bad. You want to be able to remember what went well, and to avoid making the same mistakes next time because they slipped your mind.

Go through every aspect of your sale and ask yourself how well they were executed. Did you have enough time to plan your sale, or were you frazzled as you neared the sale day? Was your advertising effective? Did your prices seem right, or did you get lots of complaints? Did you have enough help or too much help? Would you do things differently next time? If so, what would you do differently?

 **Trash or Treasure**

Stash your critique where you have your inventory stored so you know exactly

Keeping Your Selling Cap On

If you're serious about having garage sales on a regular basis, you'll need to keep thinking like a seller even when you're not selling. Always keep an eye out for inventory that you can sell. Get into the habit of storing things in a corner of your home—basement, attic, closet, garage, what have you—in preparation for your next sale, and make sure your family gets into the habit as well. After a while, putting unwanted items in your garage sale corner will become as natural as tossing them into the Dumpster once was. Watch for special sales on such items as clothes racks and other display items if you need them.

With this said, don't let garage sales take over your life. Yes, it's great to find great bargains and to make extra cash selling the things you no longer need, but it's possible to get a little too serious about it all. There aren't any self-help groups for garage sale junkies (that we know of, anyway) so it's up to you to keep things in perspective. Keep it fun, keep it enjoyable, and you'll have many years of good garage sales ahead of you!

The Least You Need to Know

- Minimize the possibility of having shoppers show up hours or days after your sale by getting your signs down fast.
- Have a plan for items that you didn't sell. Either store them away for your next sale or donate them.
- Be sure to get a receipt for any items that you donate.
- Use what you learned from your last garage sale to help plan for the next one.

Pricing Index

The following is a list of items commonly offered at garage sales and suggested price ranges for easy reference. As mentioned throughout the book, many factors—including age, condition, and demand—should be considered when pricing used goods. Because of this, there is no definitive pricing or value guide for these items, and the list that follows should in no way be considered the only recommendation. Use it as part of your pricing process, and especially if you're stuck on a specific item or items and want to get a general idea of what they often go for.

Always remember that your objective when holding a garage sale is to make money, not to give your items away. If you plan and orchestrate your sale properly, there won't be any need to fire sale your inventory. On the other hand, it's also a good idea to price your items somewhat aggressively unless you don't mind hanging on to them.

If you have items that are considered collectible, such as Barbie dolls, sports cards, rare LPs, costume jewelry from the 1940s and 1950s, etc., think twice about including them in your sale. Collectors regularly scour garage sales looking for great deals on these items, but you'll get more money for them if you sell them through other means. Always check a current collectibles price guide for their value regardless of where you decide to sell them.

Action figures: 25¢ to $1.50

Bikes: $15 to $35

Books: hardbound 50¢ to $2; paperbacks: 10 to 50¢

Cassette tapes: 50 to 75¢

CD players (portable): $2 to $5

CDs: $1 to $2

Clothing: adult, roughly 10 percent of replacement value; children's clothing: jackets 50¢ to $2; two-piece outfits $1.50 to $3; dresses $1.50 to $3; pants and overalls 50¢ to $1; shirts 25¢ to $1

Computer equipment: 5 to 25 percent of cost (if in working order and relatively new)

Computer games and software: 25 to 50 percent of cost (use the higher end of the scale if software is current)

Cosmetics and perfume: new, never used, and still in the box: 50 percent of replacement value Used: 10 to 25 percent of replacement value depending on how much product is left

Craft items: 25 to 50 percent of cost

Dishware: dishes (setting for four) $3 to $5; not matched 10¢ to $1 each

Electronic instructional books: 25 percent of cost

Fisher-Price toys, electronic toys, and video games: 25 percent of cost

Flatware (setting for four): $2 to $5

Furniture: $5 to $150

Games: 50¢ to $3

Glassware: miscellaneous glasses, not matched 10¢ to $1 each; wine glasses 25¢ to $1 each

Kitchen appliances (toaster ovens, microwaves, blenders, mixers, etc.): ¼ of cost if in working order

Kitchen gadgets (graters, slicers, manual can openers, etc.): 25 to 50¢

Lamps: $5 to $25

Linens: 50¢ to ¼ of cost

LPs: 50¢ to $1

Picture frames: 25¢ to $3

Pots and pans: 50¢ to $3

Power tools: 25 to 50 percent of cost

Radios: $1 to $4

Sporting goods: 20 to 30 percent of cost

Stuffed animals: 25¢ to $10

Television sets: black-and-white $10 to $20; color $25 to $50

Towels: 50¢ to $2

Tricycles: $1 to $8

VCRs: $15 to $25

Videotapes: $1 to $3

Resources

Check the following print and online resources for more information on garage and yard sales.

Print Resources

Huxford, Sharon and Bob. *Garage Sale and Flea Market Annual: Cashing in on Today's Lucrative Collectibles Market*. Collector Books. Published annually, this book offers advice on recognizing great buys, reselling items at the best prices, or holding your own successful sales.

Huxford, Sharon and Bob. *Schroeder's Antiques Price Guide*. Schroeder Publishing Co., Inc. A comprehensive price guide covering almost 500 antiques and collectibles categories. Published annually.

Schroy, Ellen T. and Don Johnson. *Warman's Flea Market Price Guide, 2nd Edition*. 2001, Warman Publishing Company. Although more oriented for flea market shopping, this price guide covers values on 700 hot collectibles categories. Also includes reproduction alerts and collecting trend reports. A third edition is scheduled for release in June 2003.

Online Resources

www.g-sale.com. Listings of garage sales, yard sales, and moving sales. Searchable by city and state.

www.garagesaledaily.com. Free site with daily listings of garage sales across the United States. Searchable by state, keyword, date, and zip code. Also classified ads for art and craft shows, festivals, auctions, and antique shows.

www.garagesalehunter.com. Free postings of garage sales and a searchable database of national sale listings.

www.localyardsales.com. A site for Canadian yard sales, searchable by province, county, district, and region.

www.luv2bid.com. Auction listing and garage sale information.

www.midwestrummage.com. Although the name implies that this site only covers rummage sales in the Midwest, it actually provides coverage throughout most of the United States and Canada. State by state directory, also directory listings for arts and crafts, flea markets and swap meets, antiques and collectibles, general merchandise, etc.

www.myfrontyard.com. Online search engine for garage, moving, estate, tag and yard sales. Listings searchable by distance, dates, and keywords.

www.tourdekalb.com/yardsale.htm. Three southern states—Alabama, Kentucky, and Tennessee—are home to what is billed as the world's longest yard sale, boasting more than 5,000 yard sale vendors annually along a 450-mile route from DeKalb, Alabama, to Covington, Kentucky. This site will tell you all you need to know about the annual event (with a strong focus on the Alabama portion) and help you plan your trip should you want to experience it for yourself.

www.yardsalequeen.com. This information-packed website features tips on buying and selling at yard and garage sales, links to other sale sites, message boards and chats, stories about garage sale customers, and more. Chris Heiska, the owner of the site, is an expert yard-saler (read her bio on the website to find out more) and provided many of the Insider Information sidebars in this book.

www.yardsalesearch.com. Another free listing site with listings organized by state. Also features a free sign maker for building your own yard sale signs.

Index

T–U–V

W–X–Y–Z